HEATHER H

An Anthology
of Works by;

Francis Sitwell
The Rev. Bro. Adam
Colin Weightman
William Hamilton
&
Peter Schollick

Compiled and originally published by Ian Copinger.

NORTHERN BEE BOOKS
Scout Bottom Farm, Mytholmroyd, West Yorkshire
www.northernbeebooks.co.uk

HEATHER HONEY - An Anthology of Works.

Compiled by Ian Copinger.

All rights reserved. No part of this publication may be reproduced, stored in a retrieval system, transmitted in any form or by any means electronic, mechanical, including photocopying, recording or otherwise without prior consent of the copyright holders.

ISBN: 978-1-908904-90-4

Published by Northern Bee Books, 2016

Scout Bottom Farm
Mytholmroyd
Hebden Bridge
HX7 5JS (UK)

www.northernbeebooks.co.uk

Tel: 01422 882751

HEATHER HONEY

An Anthology
of Works

PREFACE

As a hobbyist bookbinder and publisher I have, over the years, obtained permission from various copyright holders to republish the following works on heather honey.

The individual card back books have appeared at local associations either in their libraries or as occasional raffle prizes.

Because I like 'making books' I have put them all together including one by Peter Schollick specially written for this book.

Ian Copinger.

CONTENTS

HEATHER HONEY BY FRANCIS SITWELL 7
    Foreword 9
    Heather Honey 11

SOME POINTS ON HEATHER HONEY
BY REV. BRO. ADAM 31
    Introduction 33
    Strain 34
    Sections 34
    Building up Stocks for the Moor 36
    Annual Re-Queening 37
    Heather Hives 38
    Drifting 42
    Shelter 43
    Dartmoor 43
    Ericaceae 45
    Subsoil 47
    Swaling 47
    Altitude 48
    Climatic Conditions 48
    Duration of Honey-Flows 49
    Feeding 49
    Extracting 50
    Filing Machine 53
    Heather Honey 54

HEATHER HONEY BY COLIN WEIGHTMAN 57
Introduction 59
Hives 63
Colony Illustration 67
Best Bees 70
Problems on the Moors 72
Removal of the Crop 73
Exhibiting Honey 75
Marketing Honey 75
Shrimp Brood 75
Control of Varroa Destructor 76
Labelling of Honey 76

THE ART OF BEEKEEPING BY WILLIAM HAMILTON 79
Heather Honey Production 81
Description of the Heather 81
Difficulties of Producing Heather Honey 83
Methods of Preparing Colonies 83
Stages of Production Diagram 84
The Hive 87
Transporting the Bees 87
The Site 88
Management at the Moors 89
General Notes 89
Points to Remember 91

HEATHER HONEY BY PETER SCHOLLICK 93
Preface 95
Acknowledgements 96
The Seasons 97
Working for a Surplus of Heather Honey 99
What are the Considerations for a Good Heather Stance? ... 101
When is the Right Time to Move to the Heather Moors? 102
Which Types of Hives for the Moor? 103

Preparing to Move the Bees to the Heather Moors 105
Transportation 106
The Early Period of the Heather Stance Visit 109
On the Moor - Foraging for the Heather Honey 110
Foraging Over for the Season 110
Enjoy the Heather Moors 111
A Moors Bonus Number One 113
A Moors Bonus Number Two 114
Benefits of the Bees Working for Heather Honey 115
Variations Experienced when Working for Heather Honey 115
Possible Occurrences whilst the Bees are on the Moors 117
Heather and its Harvest - Types of Heather Plant 117
My Methods for Working the Bees to Obtain the Heather Honey 118
Working for Heather Honey or Heather Blend 119
Honeys Obtained and Methods of Dealing with any Crop 120
Square Sections and Round Sections 121
Colonies that have been on the Moors 122
Overview from Bee books and Related Publications. 122

HEATHER HONEY
by
FRANCIS SITWELL

This paper was first published in the British Bee Journal in April 1912.

The editor, Cecil C. Tonsley, BEM, FRES., kindly gave me permission to re-publish it.

Printed and published by Ian Copinger, Durham. 1994.

ISBN 0 9516899 7 5

FOREWORD

Francis Honorious Sisson Sitwell was born at Azamgargh, Nr. Allahabad, India in 1861. The son of Major Sitwell of Barmoor Castle, Lowick, Northumberland, he was educated at Harrow. Francis Sitwell first married in 1889 and in 1896 he took as his second wife, Margaret Elizabeth Culley, the daughter of one of Northumberland's great agricultural figures. Mathew Culley of Coupland Castle. Francis Sitwell lived at various times in Wooler, Ord Hill and Alnwick.

At the beginning of the century Francis Sitwell became Honorary Secretary of the old Northumberland B.K.A. which had been formed in 1887, and was a council member of the B.B.K.A. between 1911 and 1914. In 1912 the illustrious Dr. Cowan, father figure of the B.B.K.A., and author of many editions of the British Beekeepers Guide book, invited Sitwell to London to tell the Southerners about heather honey. It is not generally realised that many beekeepers in the South of England claimed that honey off the heather moors was just the food of peasants and were most contemptuous of the product in both conversation and writing. Single handed Major Sitwell resolved to put this right when he gave his paper to the B.B.K.A. conversazione, and from then onwards the production of heather honey off the vast heather moors of the British Isles became respectable and was viewed in a very different light.

With the outbreak of World War 1 the Northumberland B.K.A. lost a talented Hon. Secretary and by 1917 a combination of factors, poor summers, hard winters and the ravages of Isle of Wight disease

(Acarine Infestation) brought about the demise of the Association. Northumberland was without an association for almost 20 years. In 1936 the present Northumberland B.K.A. was re-launched at Hexham. In 1922 the N.E. Durham B.K.A. was renamed the Newcastle and District B.K.A. to fill the void.

Fortunately Major Sitwell survived the Great War and in later years lived at Bell View, Percy Terrace, Alnwick, where he was a local magistrate. He was also a life member and expert of the B.B.K.A. Friends who remember the Major have described him as a robust gentleman with white hair and florid cheeks who had a pleasant but formidable disposition.

After 80 years, Francis Sitwell's paper on Heather Honey is still full of interest and his thoughts about the conditions required for nectar secretion on the various moors still ring true today.

Ian Copinger must be commended for making it available to today's beekeepers.

Colin Weightman,
February 1994.

HEATHER HONEY

In selecting my subject, I did so with a specific object, namely, that discussion may possibly throw some light on many puzzling points, and thereby something may be added to our knowledge of the subject of the secretion of nectar, the cause of variations in colour, density, etc, in honey, by beekeepers who are present giving us the result of any observations they have made, or by inducing some who have time and opportunity to take notes in the future on some of the points that I shall now attempt to bring forward.

As all British bee-keepers know, heather honey is in some districts the main crop of the year. In guide books, clover is stated to be the mainstay of the bee-keeper. This may be the case in the South and Midlands, but in the North generally, and in the North of Scotland, heather, and heather alone, is all we have to depend on. In my own district, flower and clover honey are acceptable, and we try to get as much as we can; but what we aim at and work for almost entirely is to have as many stocks as possible fit and ready for the moors; in short, what we look to for our profits is the heather-crop.

Luckily for us, heather honey always commands a good price. I say luckily, for although clover years vary, one season like the last being exceptionally good and another not so good, I think I can safely state as a fact that the average clover flow is of longer duration and much more regular than the heather flow. The heather crop also varies year by year, but seldom or never in the best year does the flow last as long as the clover flow. Last year, which was quite exceptional as a whole, it barely lasted three weeks. I am talking now of the flow, not the length of time the bloom lasts. On an average it seldom lasts ten days, and what makes it extremely difficult for the beekeeper is that it comes by fits and starts, is very irregular generally, though not always, as I shall show later, coinciding with the hot days or a hot spell. With an irregular flow we all know what constant and careful watching is required to obtain the best results, and that in the home apiary; but hives at the moor are practically out apiaries, and it is seldom possible for the owner to be always on the spot, so perforce he has to trust to luck.

As samples of flows let me take the last six seasons. In 1906 the heather was in bloom about August 12th, but owing to cold and rain no honey was stored till the 30th. On that date the weather became suddenly hot, and remained so for 9 days, the temperature in the shade reaching 85°. A severe frost on the night of September 7th ended the flow as suddenly as it began. In 1907 it lasted a week, and that not until the second week in September, from 6th to 12th. In 1908 there was a very good flow from August 3rd till the 14th. After that date, nothing. In 1909 it was most uncertain, the flow being on August 27th and September 2nd, 3rd, and 5th. Only 4 days in all! In 1910 a good flow from about August 19th till 27th. On the 27th, luckily for myself I took off 48 good sections for show purposes. All racks were rapidly nearing completion, and second racks required. But alas! on the 28th the weather changed; on the 29th we had a heavy thunderstorm, followed by a week's rain and wind, which spoilt the bloom. I could not touch my hives again until September 4th, when I found the bees taking down the honey as fast as they could, so I only saved some nine or ten sections per hive, and those not saleable. I had, however, any amount of drawn out sections and baits, which came in useful this last season. In 1911 the flow was from the end of July till August 20th. Owing to the second crop of clover being exceptionally good and the heather early, they overlapped, so that a great deal of blend was obtained. Against this, the heather flow continued, and second and third racks of pure heather honey were obtained.

Now this brings me to one of the curious points wherein heather differs so greatly from clover, sainfoin, limes or other sources of nectar. By heather honey, in the North certainly, and, I fancy, in most places, it is understood to be the honey produced by the bees from the nectar secreted in common ling (Calluna vulgaris). "Its consistency is peculiar to it alone; it does not run out when cut, for the contents of each cell are distinct hexagonals of delicate jelly. Its smell and flavour, which the uninitiated consider strong, are those of the aromatic odour of flowering ling. Its colour is a wonderful amber, which is brought into marked contrast by the surrounding snowy-white opaque cell walls and cappings." There is also a honey produced from bell heather nectar (Erica cinerea). A sealed section of the one, to look at only, cannot be distinguished from a sealed section of the other. The experiment has been tried by the Northumberland and Durham B.K.A. in Newcastle, but, on cutting, the veriest novice could tell the difference; to use a common expression, they are "as different as chalk from cheese." Bar the colour and whiteness of capping, there was no comparison. The bell heather sample had not the same smell; it ran freely when cut, and when tasted was pronounced a flower honey. As is well known, ling honey cannot be extracted, whereas that from bell heather extracts more easily than clover. In this instance, and in others, there was no difference in the colour of the two samples; but I have also evidence that it is often very much lighter in colour. I wonder whether the two species of Erica account for this (E. tetralix and E. cinerea). Now we come to a strange fact. That ling honey, or, as we call it, heather honey, varies both in flavour and colour North and South of the Tweed, is well known, that farther North being reputed stronger in flavour and darker in colour than that farther South. But the Tweed is not the boundary line. Mr. Avery, the well known Sec. of the Cumberland and Westmorland B.K.A. writing to me, says: "I may say it varies considerably in colour and density in different parts of the counties, and., except on some of the lower hills, is not so dense as that from the Cheviots. The flavour and aroma, however, are quite equal to any except that gathered on some of the more Northern Scottish hills." Again Dr. Moore-Ede (Medicus), whose interesting observations and experiments at the moors are well known to all readers of the Bee Journal, assures me that my honey from the foot of Cheviot is much stronger than his from Edmundbyers in the South of the county. He has also noticed a difference in strength and colour in honey from two moors, one ten miles North and the other ten miles South of the Tyne. I could go on quoting other instances where these variations have been observed. There is evidently no hard and fast dividing line, such as the Tweed; but how are we to account for these variations?

So far, I have only touched on the differences in colour, flavour and density in heather honey obtained from various moors, if we can hold the moors responsible. But now we come to a much more important difference. Two sets of moors, though only a few miles apart, may have very different values to the beekeeper as regards his heather crop. For instance take in my own district: Wooler may be described as lying on the North-east corner of the foothills of old Cheviot himself. Moor after moor rise one behind the other to the South and West. Across the valley of the Till lie a belt of moors, partly on a sandstone outcrop, and partly with a clay subsoil. Beyond these, again, is a long, comparatively low line of moors, on whinstone, commencing at Kyloe, opposite Holy Island and running almost due South for some twenty miles. If a stranger went from one set of moors to the others he would find it hard to select the best as regards the quantity of bloom on the ling. Yet no Wooler beekeeper would ever dream of sending his stocks across the valley , though the roads are good. No he sends them up awful roads to the Cheviot moors. The beekeepers across the vale, with ling at their very doors, also send to the Cheviots. Why? I have asked members of my Association, and the answer has been : It's no use your sending to the whinstone." The subsoil has always been held accountable for the difference in results, and the value of the two sets of moors, from the beekeeper's point of view, viz., profits. I may mention that the

Cheviots are augite granite. I thought " They had reason," as the French say, founded on experience, until I received a letter from Mr. McNally, whose letters in the Record we all know and appreciate, and who is essentially a "heather man". He tells me that all his honey is gathered on whinstone moors! Glenluce, where he lives is almost exactly 150 miles due South-west from Wooler in a bee-line. Mr. McNally's bees work at about 500ft. above sea level, and he is only a few miles from the sea. The Kyloe moors, which our beekeepers count of such little value, are only a few miles from the sea, and run from 400ft to 700ft above sea level. What we fail to get on the East coast Mr. McNally gets - and obtains in paying quantity, moreover on the West! The conditions are apparently the same, but the results are very different. Mr. Avery, writing also of the West, considers the whinstone yields the best quality". Why? Has our old friend "the Gulf Stream" got something to say to this result? Now I will give you an instance where the subsoil is clearly the chief factor. A Yorkshire friend writes; "The chalk marl and limestone sides of our dales are much preferred to the sides with sandstone subsoil. We get the finest grade from the ironstone subsoil and the finest flavour in existence. The density is one solid jelly." Many old beekeepers say that heather on freestone or sandstone produces honey freely; but the quality is inferior to that from whinstone or limestone, though the quantity is, as a rule, greater. What is the reason?

As a surface soil, peat seems to be a necessity for the growth of heather. That heather and heaths both grow best in a peaty soil there is no doubt. The greater the depth of peat the better and stronger the plant, and in consequence the more nectar secretion. Where there is only a few inches of peat on the surface there does not appear to be much nectar secreted in either heather or heaths.

Talking to a beekeeper the other day, he suggested that drainage had a great deal to do with this question of variableness in heather honey. At the moment we were discussing the poor value of a neighbouring moor, but as the subsoil was clay, my gardener friend's theory that "want of drainage meant cold, and drainage warmth, thereby affecting the secretion of nectar in ling" was probably correct in this particular case; and it is borne out by some notes from Ayrshire. There the moors yielding best results are some 1200ft above sea-level, on limestone with a good dry surface. From some bogland moors, about 700ft up, with wet, boggy surface, the results are not nearly so good, the honey differing in density, colour and flavour in two cases. Again, in Aberdeen-shire, the darker, stronger honey is from the high moors, the lower wet moors yielding a much poorer quality. One very experienced heather man from Yorkshire (Whitby district) says, "The higher and drier the moors the better the yield. The low moist parts of the moor never, to my knowledge, yield any honey",

That there is a great deal in this theory I am convinced, for "a wet season makes a sample lacking in consistency." are the words of a well known authority, "D.M.M., Banff." A beekeeper who sends to the Berwickshire moors gives "a friable loamy clay" as his ideal for a sub-soil for the heather plant or shrub. This question of drainage I think should be taken in conjunction with the growth of the plant itself when seeking for the reasons for the variations in the honey. There are three distinct styles of growth to be noted in ling: First, a dry scrub which flowers fairly well but yields a small supply; second, a tall, rank growth in damp places and on low-lying moors, which gives a very poor return, and the sample is thin, watery, and of poor keeping quality; third, the ling at its best--miles, aye leagues, of the famous purple heather. Purple, the royal colour befitting our most regal honey.

Drainage, therefore, has a good deal to do with good results, but with drainage, so to speak, equal subsoils play an important part. Granite is, beyond all question, always excellent. Ironstone and gritstone have strong claims to be considered among the best. Whinstone, as I have shown, seems to give different results on the East and West Coasts, though it is admittedly better than sandstone, and probably better than limestone. Chalk marl and limestone seem better than sandstone, while a loamy clay has a good claim as an excellent sub-soil. But even now I don't think we have got to the bed rock of what is the real reason why some heather honey is so very much better than other.

Altitude would seem to be a very important factor in obtaining the best results, but here again we are met by much conflicting evidence. In Cumberland and Westmorland it is stated that the best quality of heather honey in the two counties is secured from the lower ranges, that from higher up on the mountains is lighter in colour and not so dense. Notes from Berwickshire support this view. To the contrary, in the Cheviot and Tweed Borders, Ayrshire and Aberdeenshire, the North of Scotland, Derbyshire, and Yorkshire, and elsewhere, there is a consensus of opinion that the best and purest ling honey comes from the high moors. One friend is very emphatic on the point. He says "altitude is a most important factor in securing the very best sample. Heather, even if abundant and showing a wealth of bloom, does not give genuine heather honey below, say, 500ft., and gives the best when grown at over 1000ft. Derbyshire (Peak district), the lower stretches of Banffshire and Aberdeenshire, to take some samples, yield honey lacking in density, flavour and aroma. The honey in some of these cases is darker and duller. My Ayrshire friend describes the honey from the lower wet moors in that county as "muddy". On some of the Derbyshire moors, which run on unbrokenly into Yorkshire, however, the honey is described as "very dense (jelly-like) rather bright, not quite so dark as some Scotch." But these moors are from 800ft. to 1000ft. up. The Yorkshireman's summary, "the higher and drier the better the yield," I have quoted before.

Now, may I touch on the subject of the granulation of heather honey? I have never seen my own do so, but perhaps it never gets the chance-it is eaten too quickly. A lady in my neighbourhood lays by large stores of it at a time, and keeps it for years, and she only occasionally finds it granulated. One heather man says, "I have kept a section for two years by putting it on a plate and covering with a basin, cutting it in two, and laying it on its side on the plate, and it was absolutely free from granulation with no running on the plate, but just the same as if taken from a hive. I have kept two sections for five years with slight granulation." Another, with 25 years experience, says "pure heather honey, 100%., will hardly granulate at all." Mr. McNally says it will granulate if kept in a low temperature (both comb and pressed). "D.M.M." says "well ripened heather honey does not candy readily." A man whose opinion I value says of granulation: The levulose never; after about 6 months the dextrose will granulate in large granules and leave the levulose liquid, having then the appearance of golden syrup mixed with rough oatmeal. I have often seen sections that exactly answered to this description. Pressed honey in some seasons seem to granulate fairly quickly, and has also been noticed to decrease rapidly in bulk when cold weather comes on. Pressed heather honey also varies in colour and consistency, as the following description will show. One lot is described as "a muddy-brown; it is deficient in density so much so that when pressed and put in bottles no air bubbles are retained in the honey, and of course flavour is lacking." Whereas the other is described as being "of a bright, sparkling amber, density and flavour first class, and altogether quite a different article; also, when good honey is pressed and put into bottles, a great quantity of air-bubbles are retained, making it look like soft soap." A good honey, when pressed, may be said to fall in lumps rather than run.

Now here is another case of the contradictiousness of heather honey. Granulation is considered a sign of purity in honey. But is it so with ling honey? One heather man goes so far as to say, "My opinion is heather honey, really pure, will not granulate at all, and heather honey generally so called pure is not really so, and the less pure the more the granulation." He is corroborated by many. "The least mixture of mustard which blooms at the same time as the ling will cause all honey to granulate very quickly. A mixture of any other will also cause it to granulate smoothly" is the result of observation in Yorkshire. That an early heather flow does not yield heather honey of the purest, because other sources of nectar are available at the same time, is true - witness last season. One wise man prefers to send to extra high moors, to avoid the risk of his bees gathering from other sources. Granulation gradually increasing according to the amount of other than heather in the cells seems to sum up the results of many observations. Anyone can test this by sampling a section of heather-blend that has been kept some time; the ling portion will be found liquid, while the flower parts of it will be granulated. Regarding re-liquefying granulated heather honey, Bro. Columban, of candy fame, whose skill nobody will dispute, notes that heather honey does not behave like other honeys when re-liquefied. It loses both mellowness and consistency.

Heather honey as a winter food seems to be a vexed question lately started in the "B.B.J." Some declare it is deadly, others that it is excellent as such. I think that it only adds one more to the many puzzles that a study of heather honey confronts one with. In some localities, and with certain grades of heather honey, it may a bad winter food, but most assuredly in others it has been for years the staple store, with no ill effects.

Let me now take some other perplexing points regarding the secretion of nectar in ling. What would be called and rightly considered a good working day for other flows may prove the reverse on the moors, and vice versa. It has been proved that ling secretes nectar at a very low temperature; bees will gather nectar if procurable, and consequently often commence work with the thermometer only registering 48deg. or less. One can watch them coming home with distended abdomens, proving that a flow is on, but, alas! many fall short, get chilled, and never rise again. When the sky is completely overcast with clouds, bees work freely all day, not even stopping for light rain; but on a bright day, whenever heavy clouds obscure the sun temporarily, they rush off home; the result is broken time and a loss on the intake. Bees at the moors seem very sensitive to these conditions. One year it was noticed that the flow only kept bees busy between the hours of 8 a.m. and 10 a.m. On the same moor the following year bees worked all day long. Both were bad years. In both the climatic conditions were nearly the same - cold northerly winds, the air humid, and evaporation very slow. The first year the wind was mainly from the N.W. , the second year mainly from the N.E. How can we account for the difference in the hours of nectar secretion?

One careful observer thinks that nectar is only secreted under certain humid conditions; and, judging the flow by the bees' work, states that the bees work early to late, but mid-day predominates. Another, whom I envy, because he spends his holidays with his bees on the moors, sums up a long experience and some very careful observation in the sentence, "Everything depends on the airt of the wind." His version of the old fishing rhyme has a great deal of truth in it.

"When the wind is in the North, Then the bee goeth not forth; When the wind is in the South, It blows the nectar into the bee's mouth; When the wind is in the East, There's much hard flying, but no real feast; When the wind is in the West, Then the flow is at its best."

He pins his faith for the nectar flow to heat: "Then the inevitable and glorious heat wave comes along - five, six or seven days - and the harvest is secured." Heat with a south or west wind is the desire of his heart.

Most beekeepers, I imagine, would not expect much of a flow on seeing the ground white from a heavy hoar frost, and the temperature never above 58deg. all day; certainly they would not expect a flow until the sun had warmed things up a bit. Yet on such a day a hive on scales gained 10lbs. between eight and ten in the morning; after ten o'clock the flow ceased. A frost in this case did no harm, but elsewhere it has been noted to have harmful effects. "Honey from low lying moors is not nearly so good, from the fact that early frosts often settle in low lying places while the higher ground is quite free, this often accounts for a sudden stoppage of work, though to all appearances the weather and bloom is all that could be desired." One very cold year, with clover in bloom close to the hives, the bees worked at the ling but would not look at the clover. Last year, which was a very hot one, some beekeepers, with their stocks near the edges of the moors, got nothing but a clover-heather blend! Does this prove that heat is a necessity for the secretion of nectar in clover? With an intermittent heather flow bees will work at clover when the ling is not secreting, but seem to prefer the ling if obtainable.

Other factors to be taken into consideration, regarding the quantity and quality of heather honey, are sunshine, exposure, and shelter. What I mean by this is, the heather should be exposed to the sun, the hives should be in the midst of the heather if possible, but the hives themselves must be sheltered. Sunshine is needed to ripen the bloom, and help in the secretion of nectar, for there is not the smallest doubt that a heat wave is conducive to a good flow, and it is generally, though as I have shown not always, on the hot days, whether continuous or with intervals, that the crop is secured. A stance in a valley gives shelter, and the laden bees can float down to their homes instead of having to struggle uphill. If on a level upland moor, or plateau, hives should be placed within "stells" (circular walled-in enclosures for sheltering sheep), which will protect them from the wind at all events. Regarding sunshine, valleys running East and West claim one advantage over those running North and South, and that is that the bloom lasts longer. The slopes facing towards the South are first covered with bloom. After a distinct interval those to the North burst into bloom. This means a longer heather season, with a greater chance of securing a late flow should it come along. As one of my members described a certain moor: "It is favoured in having two crops." In a valley running North and south, one slope gets the morning sun, and the other the evening sun, while both get the midday sunshine; but the bloom on both slopes alike, begins and ends about the same time.

A sentence of "D.M.M.'s," in an old paper he kindly lent me, I think deserves attention. Writing on this point of sunshine, he claims that heather facing South or S.W. yields better returns, and, he is inclined to think, "a better quality of nectar." Has the subject of the quality of nectar, as affecting honey, been investigated? If it has, I apologise for my ignorance; if it has not, is it not worthy of research?

It may lie at the root of the mystery. For instance, some heather men account for ling honey this last season being rather lighter in colour than usual from the fact that the drought checked the blooms coming fully out. The blooms not being fully developed might possibly result in the nectar not being properly protected, therefore not so well ripened. Could Prof. Bonnier's opinion on this point be obtained?

As far as I can gather, in the North and Midlands, In Scotland and Ireland Ericas or heaths are repudiated as a source of supply, only being found in small quantities on the moors. By the way, two a least of my members challenge whether bee; can gather the nectar in bell heather at all They have lived all their lives on the moors and have never seen our little friends touch Ericas. In Devonshire, however, on the lower stretches of Dartmoor, heaths and heather both abound; but as the moors rise the ling predominates. A great deal of this Dartmoor honey is blend, though the true jelly like heather honey is obtained also, but it is no equal to the heather honey of Scotland an the North. From Somerset I gather that large quantities of heather (almost entirely bell heather) grow on Exmoor and the Quantocks and a little on the Mendips. The two former run to over 1000ft. - sub soil chiefly of red sandstone. Heather blend is obtained in fair quantity on the southern slopes of the Quantocks, and the valley between them, an Exmoor. The crop, however, is uncertain, and it is not considered profitable to move bee to the heather districts. Very little surplus is obtained on the Mendips. Insufficiency of pasturage within easy reach, absence of ling and stocks not properly prepared, are three very good reasons to account for this. As the heather honey of Somerset is usually mixed with that from other sources, it is seldom so thick that it cannot go through the extractor.

Notes from Ireland corroborate most of the points noted elsewhere. Igneous basic rocks, locally called greenstone, furnish good subsoil. The heather grows right to the summits of the mountains, and we should call them high moors, the more outlying glens producing the stronger and darker honey. Pressed honey granulates fairly quickly, but comb honey properly kept will hardly granulate. Ireland adds her quota to the conundrum list. Can anyone explain why, last season of all others, heather sections, though well sealed and ripe, were extremely light in weight, not well filled at all? Also why "in the last two years the heather honey was not nearly as dark as usual in colour?" The altitude, subsoil, drainage etc., could not have suddenly changed, but the colour of the honey did! Why?

Before closing my paper, may I touch on the subject of heather honey on the show bench? I have shown that ling honey is absolutely distinct from bell heather honey although we find them both commonly designated heather honey, and in honey competitions both sorts are usually shown in the same class. Is this quite fair? Botanists tell us of the many differences between the two. "The extensive genus Erica (heath) contains no plant possessing useful properties. Calluna vulgaris (ling or heather) is astringent, and is sometimes used for dyeing." As plants they all vary. "Linnaeus placed both in the genus Erica (heath); but later botanists have, however, made of it a distinct genus, and not without reason." To begin with, there is only one species of ling or heather, while there are two common E. tetralix (cross-leaved heath), largish pink bells, and E. cinerea (fine leaved heath), smaller magenta bells, and several more rare species of heaths. Their outward differences are apparent to the eye of any beekeeper, while the beekeeper who is also a botanist can tell us that they vary as much as the Bombi differ from Apis Mellifica. Heaths flower and the honey is stored some weeks earlier than ling honey, and therefore under more favourable climatic conditions; the farther south the better these conditions. Taking all this into consideration, would it not be quite possible to have separate classes for the two varieties of honey? Heather honey from ling has a consistency, flavour, and aroma of its own, quite distinctive from all others. That from heaths, except in colour, and that not always, has not the faintest resemblance to it. It tastes, and extracts like a flower honey. Why class them together? The careless use of the word heather, I suppose, had something to do with it. Call the latter heath honey if you like, Erica honey would sound rather strange perhaps, but Bell-heather Honey would look fine on a label! But do not call it heather-honey.

In the same way, I think a very clear distinction should be drawn between the genuine article and blends. Because a hive happens to be on a moor, it does not follow the bees are working only at the ling. Wild thyme, heaths, or even clover may be within reach, and the nectar in them being secreted simultaneously. More care should be taken in classifying for the show bench. Blends should be in a class of their own. Honey from ling, and ling alone, I think, should have the title of heather honey. Heather men in the North I am pretty certain would vote solid for this claim of our main-crop, and of what we believe to be the finest honey there is.

Mr. Herrod, in one of his "Helpful Hints," and very helpful they are, gave three mistakes that young beekeepers fall into, and I feel very much as if I have been sadly guilty of the third, for I cannot claim a third of the experience that he had before he began to write on bee subjects. But please remember I am not pretending to lay down any laws on the subject of heather honey. It has been a labour of love to collect data from all parts of the kingdom, on facts; and I leave it to wiser and more experienced beekeepers to deduce theories from them. Before some of these problems are solved, I think, we shall have to call in the assistance of both botanists and geologists, but in the meantime I trust that beekeepers may find them interesting.

If I may briefly summarise, the only points that appear at all clear in my own mind are: That heather and heaths should not be mixed up; that blends should be acknowledged as such; that to account for the many variations in colour, flavour, and density, we must study subsoil, drainage, altitudes, the lie of the land re sunshine and exposure, also the plant itself; but to get the best ling honey, we must look to a pure source of supply more than anything. That is, one in which the bees cannot get at any other source of nectar. This would account for the many claims for a high altitude. It will probably be found, I think, that where and when, what those of us who know and love it call "the genuine article," is obtained, other sources of supply will befound absent, and the result is, the amber jelly that does not run, with the aromatic taste and aroma of the ling from which our little friends draw the nectar, the true heather honey.

I beg to acknowledge the valuable assistance I have received from many personal friends, and from heathermen generally from all parts, and now tender them my very best thanks.

The Chairman said they had had an excellent paper by Captain Sitwell, for which they were indebted to him, and called upon any of those present to give their experience on the subject.

Mr. Crawshaw said he felt that Captain Sitwell had covered the field, but he had several observations to make. Regarding the characteristics of heather honey produced at the different moors, he felt that possibly by investigation of the tabulation of the results in a complete manner it might be possible to arrive at some conclusion. He thought if the information was really obtained the differences would be found not to depend entirely upon the subsoil; we might find the weather to vary the result. Usually, in his district, the Erica cinerea flow runs fairly close to the beginning of the Calluna vulgaris flow, and the weather conditions may make them overlap. The colour and consistency are certainly affected when they do overlap: the colour is dark and the consistency thinner. To get the bees to take to supers he sent sections to the moors from which he had just extracted clover honey. He found it a mistake to send foundation in the sections. Referring to the granulation of heather honey, he said it does occur in what appeared to be heather honey, as he found that uncapped cells in which the honey was exposed granulated very much more readily than when protected. The granulation was course, quite unlike that of clover honey. In heather honey from a millstone grit subsoil, he found quite 50% rejected by the bees when feeding on account of granulation. As to the suitability of heather honey as a winter food for bees, he thought it just possible that they may become "acclimatised" to the conditions. He supported the suggestion that ling honey should be classed separately, as there is no comparison between the two kinds. He accused Southern judges of knowing very little about the subject, and suggested inviting them to the moors to see for themselves. During his experience he had found honey-dew often put up as heather honey, and wondered if it was supplied by some inexperienced person. When on a visit to Mr. Quayle, in the Isle of Man, he found that gentleman taking shallow combs of heather honey, putting them into the extractor, and slinging the honey out like water, and that same honey was in a short time hard and granulated.

Mr. Pugh said there was a good deal of misconception as to what constituted "heather blend." Some seemed to think it should be principally clover with a dash of heather, while others held it should be heather with a dash of clover. He had won many medals with bell heather honey mixed with clover, but he found that clover honey with a dash of heather was most suited to the public taste, the bell heather honey came from the combs, as did Mr. Quayle's, but with the true heather honey it was quite impossible to remove it with the extractor. What was considered to be the correct thing on the show bench? Were the prizes to be awarded to the pure heather honey or to the sample that suited the judge's taste best? In Derbyshire they were wintering entirely on heather honey and the bees were doing well.

Mr. Reid said in Surrey large areas of land were suitable for the growth of heather. He found it would not grow at all on a calcareous soil, and he had never found it on limestone. With regard to heather grown in the South, when he first started judging many years ago, he confessed he did not know what he thought sufficient about heather honey, so he asked advice, and the reply was given him, "If you taste any honey that you would not eat yourself, that is the true heather honey." True heather honey had such a rough taste that he personally would prefer the blend. He did not know if he had ever tasted a sample of pure bell heather honey, and would like to get a sample from a place where no other flowers were blooming at the same time. In Surrey some years ago, there were complaints from exhibitors that they could not produce pure heather honey as the bees gathered from other sources at the same time, consequently heather blend classes were instituted. If we were to introduce, as Captain Sitwell suggested, a class for the bell heather honey, he thought the judge would say that all the exhibits were mixed honeys, and there would be no awards.

Formerly, everything that had the slightest taste of heather was sold as true heather honey. Regarding granulation, one is apt to look upon it from the sugar standpoint, but there is another side. In all honeys there are colloid bodies. If you mix with a crystallisable solution a small proportion of a colloid this will prevent crystallisation. The proportion of water to the sugars has a very important influence in the granulation. Heather honey as we know it is so thickened by colloids that the percentage of sugar to water may be very much smaller than in ordinary cases.

Mr. Pugh considered the taste for pure heather honey was an acquired one.

Mr. Crawshaw said Mr. Pugh referred to this as an acquired taste. There is no doubt that a heather man will hear of nothing else. As to the difference of opinion between certain beekeepers respecting different moors he thinks it is easily accounted for by the rainfall. The high moors are drier on the eastern side than on the western side, which will account for the difference.

Mr. Cowan said he admired very much the painstaking way in which Captain Sitwell collected his information: it was only information of that sort that was of any use in coming to a decision as to the qualities of heather. The taste for heather honey was undoubtedly an acquired one, and he had not inherited it, although a Scotsman. He preferred the milder southern honeys to the heather honey, and there are a great many others who hold the same view. No one on the Continent would think of eating heather honey and there they used it for making ginger bread. There are large beekeepers who produce heather honey in Germany - and Luneburg Heath beekeepers. Their bees have to winter on this honey and they manage to live through the winters successfully. The forest beekeepers in Sussex considered the mixture of heather honey was not good for wintering and that it caused dysentery. Regarding the chemical ingredients of honey, iron was a very important one, and when present it quite changed the aspect of any honey, and probably had its influence on heather honey. The subsoil also made a great difference, and he had no doubt that the sun played a very important part. The power of the sun on mackerel is known to influence their growth, and, no doubt it would have an effect on the growth of flowers and the production of nectar. Hygrometric conditions also had their influence as well as altitude and aspect. In the class for heather honey, he very often used to find exhibits of heather blend, but there were now two classes. Heather blend should be a clover honey with a dash of heather, not heather with a dash of clover. Scottish heather honey (Calluna vulgaris) is longer before it granulated. Stiff honey may be made liquid by beating, and in Germany heather honey is now being extracted by piercing the cells of the honey with thick needles so that it can be extracted in the ordinary way. It was new to him to learn that heather would flourish on a lime soil.

Mr. Till questioned if it was true that you could make heather grow where there was lime. He had transported heather from Hayes Common to Eynsford but could not get it to grow

Captain Sitwell, in replying, said he was only putting facts before them. Limestone is stated to be the subsoil of the moors in Ayshire. They say limestone subsoil will produce greater quantities of honey than sandstone, but not of such good quality. He never got bell heather honey as he took care not to send to the moors until this was over. Wild thyme is a common plant on the Cheviots, and a favourite among the beekeepers, but the taste for this honey is acquired. The quality of nectar is a question that should be studied.

SOME POINTS ON HEATHER HONEY PRODUCTION
by
REV. BRO. ADAM OF BUCKFASTLEIGH

Being extracts from the meeting of the Newcastle and District Beekeepers' Association, held in Newcastle on December 8th, 1934.

On the 8th December 1934 almost three hundred beekeepers from all over the North of England gathered at the Hancock museum in Newcastle to hear a lecture by the Rev. Bro. Adam of Buckfast on the subject of
heather honey.

The body of his talk was published by Newcastle and District Beekeepeers Association at a cost of 5gns.

First published in 1934.

The association records show a payment of £2.12.6d for refreshments at the meeting and a gratuity of 6s.0d.

The comments Bro. Adam made at this lecture are arguable as valid now as they were then. Few of the pamphlets seem to have survived the passage of time.

Limited edition of 50 copies ISBN 0 9516899 1 6

Published by Ian Copinger Durham 1990

© Newcastle and District B.K.A

INTRODUCTION

The production of heather honey is of very ancient origin. It was known to the ancient Greeks and is referred to in old legal documents in Britain, the term " herds of bees " referring to the taking of bees to the moors.

To build up a stock for a honey-flow occurring in June or July is a simple task. It is in the nature of bees to build up to develop in strength after winter is past. The heather-harvest, however, coincides with a stage in the life-cycle of a colony when preparations are m progress for maintaining its existence by rest, not activity. The problem, therefore, is to delay, to offset, if we can, premature preparations for winter. Various means calculated to attain this, are used. For instance: artificial stimulation between clover and heather harvest; doubling of colonies; strengthening by the addition of driven bees; alternatively, by contraction of the brood-nest, are some of the means resorted to counterbalance the decline in colony-strength.

It is not my intention to enlarge on expedients of this kind for preparing stocks for the moor. We endeavour to solve the difficulty under consideration by strains which maintain colony-strength until late in the season, and in the unrestricted, full development of stocks.

STRAIN

As just indicated, the variety or strain of bees kept is one of the foremost factors conducive to success in the production of honey on the moor. It must be realized that bees which do excellently early in the season will not perforce do well also on the moor. Conditions in general are vastly different during a heather honey-flow than those prevailing earlier in the season. Italians give, taking everything into consideration, the most satisfactory returns on the clover; but on the heather, especially the progeny of imported queens, fail notoriously. Carniolans too, although alpine bees, do riot, in our estimation, possess the characteristics demanded for heather honey production. We have given this variety a prolonged trial, on an extensive scale, but were eventually compelled to discard them.

We find black bees, imported from the south of France, if crossed with Italians, most excellent for the moor,

Dutch bees seem pre-eminently adapted for the production of heather honey. Here we call them " Dutch bees," but on the Continent they are known as " heath bees." The heath bee is a variety of the common brown bee. It has been evolved, in the course of hundreds of years, by the influence of moorland environments and the most intensive system of heather honey production known. Heath bees are hardy, long-lived, good comb builders, and forage almost in any weather. They are the bees exclusively developed by heather men for heather honey production. Unfortunately it is very difficult to obtain queens of the true heath bees.

SECTIONS

There seems almost an unlimited demand for heather honey in the comb. Moreover, well-tilled heather sections command the highest market price of any honey produced, either in this or any other country. Perhaps hardly any other article of food looks as attractive as heather honey in the comb. The pearly white cappings, so peculiar to heather honey, impart to sections a most exquisite delicacy of appearance.

Yet, in spite of the high price obtained, it is most difficult to produce them economically in average seasons. The problem consists not so much in getting sections tilled, as in procuring complete sealing of the combs. Heather secretes nectar in abnormally low temperatures, and when such conditions prevail, bees cannot elaborate wax for sealing combs. Indeed, in seasons of this kind, the bulk of the crop obtained is generally not sealed.

Instances are on record of takes of one hundred and eighty completed heather sections from one colony. However, such returns must be attributed to exceptional seasons, or to abnormal circumstances. Drifting probably was the cause of such takes.

In working for heather honey it is imperative lo have every section tilled with drawn comb before being taken to the moor. The reluctance manifested by bees, even under ordinary conditions, to build comb late in the season is notorious. This trait is greatly intensified on the moor owing, as already pointed out, to the low day and night temperatures which then so frequently prevail. In normal seasons it is next to impossible to get bees to draw out foundation in shallow frames on the moor, and consequently they will still much less build comb in sections.

The section-racks we use are designed to take one shallow extracting-comb on either side, with the frames holding the sections between. This arrangement, to a great measure, minimizes the number of unfinished sections; and if, when the central sections near completion, they are transposed with those next to the extracting combs, all can be got evenly filled and sealed.

When working for heather honey in shallow combs, even in the poorest seasons, some surplus is usually obtained, but to secure a remunerative crop of comb honey, a season above the average is demanded. With sections, there is the further disadvantage that all unsaleable ones have to be destroyed.

BUILDING UP STOCKS FOR THE MOOR

The crop from the heather, in nine out of ten seasons, is gathered between mid-August and September 10th. Therefore, when building up stocks destined for the moor, it is well to re-member that, from the moment an egg is deposited in a worker-cell until a bee emerges and assumes duties outside the hive, normally five weeks elapse. During the active season the life of a worker-bee usually does not exceed four weeks. Hence, from the eggs a queen lays between June 20th and July xoth will emerge the bees destined to gather the heather crop. Consequently, if from June 20th to July 10th breeding is interrupted or retarded by manipulations, swarming, re-queening, accidental loss of queen or any other cause, such colonies are bound to fail on the moor. In case a serious interruption of brood-rearing took place, during the vital building-up period, a stock may appear strong when taken to the moor, but will subsequently dwindle rapidly and prove useless for producing a surplus.

In this connection there is another aspect on which too much stress cannot be laid, namely, the detrimental after-effects to a colony of an insufficient held force to enable the incoming nectar to be stored in the supers. A weak colony usually clogs the brood-nest with honey, and thereby endangers its survival through winter by reason of an insufficiency of young bees.

I will cite a concrete instance, in illustration of what I have just stated.

Last year two otherwise successful beekeepers placed their hives close to some of our apiaries. As a matter of fact, their bees were in one of the best districts on Dartmoor. I was rather interested, for the sake of comparison, to hear, subsequently, how they fared. Both thought they had done well, for they obtained a surplus of about 27 lb. per hive. However, to my amazement, they reported that after August 12th their bees made no further gain; whereas, in reality, the heaviest flow occurred from the 25th to the 28th of August. Indeed, the flow was so heavy that our own stocks must have averaged about

14 lb. each day. The explanation is simple if you will recall what was said regarding the critical three weeks, from June 20th to July 10th, in the development of colonies destined for the production of heather honey. One of the two beekeepers mentioned, moreover, lost his bees the winter following.

Although the brood-chamber we have is the largest in use, yet we have to let our colonies run short of super room to compel them to store enough honey in the brood-nest for winter. It is a thing well worth remembering that the stronger a colony, the less the danger of an undue amount of honey finding its way into the brood-chamber—provided, of course, adequate super room is given in time.

ANNUAL RE-QUEENING

There is an idea prevalent amongst heather honey producers that, to obtain the very best results, it is necessary to re-queen each colony some time in July. However, I am led to the conclusion that it is a mistake to re-queen previous to the heather-flow—except in cases where bees are within reach of the moor from their permanent stands. Re-queening will be found beneficial then, because a young queen will keep up a brood-nest of moderate size, whereas an old queen all too frequently ceases laying immediately the heather commences to yield. But the position is quite the reverse where stocks are transported perhaps many miles to a distant moor. The jolting and general excitement caused by a journey rouses the bees to a renewed spurt of brood-rearing, to which one-year-old queens, still in their prime, respond more readily than queens only a few weeks old. We find colonies headed by one-year-old queens return from the moor in better condition for winter than either stocks which were re-queened prior to being taken to the heather, or those left on their permanent stands.

To introduce a queen of necessity entails a break in brood-rearing. A week usually elapses before a new queen is accepted and laying. Then a further two or three weeks pass by before a young queen is laying normally, and, moreover, a queen the summer she is born will never lay as well as when in her prime the year after. This, I believe, is a point not always fully appreciated.

HEATHER HIVES

The selection of a suitable type of hive, for the production of heather honey, is an item of no small importance. A heather hive must comply to the following requirements:

(1) It must be adapted for securing the hive parts and for confining the bees efficiently, with the minimum ex-penditure of time and labour.

(2) It must provide the strongest colony ample ventilation and clustering space.

(3) It must be of a size and shape to permit loading closely together on a lorry or railway truck.

(4) It must provide adequate protection to a colony against the abnormal fluctuations in temperature which usually prevail on the moor.

Most appliance dealers sell hives which are specially designed for taking bees to the moors. It would seem, however, that in the majority of patterns insufficient attention is paid lo the provision of both clustering space and ventilation. The single-walled American type of hive is admirably adapted for transportation, but hardly affords adequate protection in northern parts of Great Britain. The conventional W.B.C. hive is perfect from the point of view of protection, but entails too much extra work in transportation, where a large number of colonies are taken to the heather. For many years we successfully used the internal fittings of W.B.C. hives as temporary heather hives.

A floor-board was made for this purpose the exact outside width of a ten-frame brood-chamber, but extending three inches beyond the front to form an alighting-board. The day previous to taking the stocks to the moor, the roof and outer casings of the W.B.C. hives were removed, the brood-chamber lifted, and the temporary floor-board placed underneath it. A shallow-super, or section-rack, was then put in position over the brood-combs, and on top of the super was put a wire-gauze super clearer to provide the necessary ventilation. The separate parts composing the hive were fastened together at each corner with crate staples.

On the morning after, about five o'clock, a perforated zinc strip was slipped into the groove at either side of the doorway and secured into position along the edge of the brood-chamber with tacks. The hive was then ready for the journey. Prepared in this manner, sixty hives, including roofs, can, with ease, be accommodated on a two-and-a-half-ton lorry.

The makeshift hive I have just described was used by us for ten years. We found it had one serious drawback. The standard ton-frame brood-chamber did not provide an adequate reserve of stores in seasons when cold, wet spells prevented the secretion of nectar until September. In such seasons, stocks were all too often on the verge of starvation by the time the weather improved.

Only one satisfactory remedy suggested itself, a larger brood-chamber—a brood-chamber commensurate in comb area to two ten-frame standard brood-chambers. But the general tendency in heather honey production was rather the other way, namely, for the reduction in the size of the brood-nest to endeavour to force the highly prized heather honey into the supers. However, in our case the experimental hives, with brood-chambers of equal comb area to twenty British standard frames, in due course yielded must gratifying results on th« moor. As I have already intimated, normally *no* undue amount of honey is stored in these large brood-chambers.

The brood-chamber of the hive we use is twenty inches square, and accommodates twelve frames of Modified Dadant size. Whilst externally it resembles the American single-walled hive, it differs materially in many important details of design.

The floor-board has a slope of I in. from back to front, and the sides are rabbeted to prevent rain entering between the junction of the floor and brood-chamber. The entrance is 18 ins. wide by I in. in depth, and may be reduced with an entrance block to 12 ins. by ¼in.; the size of entrance invariably allowed on the moor. The floor-board extends only one inch beyond the front of the brood-chamber, and a detachable alighting-board is fitted instead.

Supers, both extracting and section-racks, are 6 ins. deep, and accommodate either ten extracting combs, or alternatively, two extracting combs and eight section frames, each holding four 4 x 5 no bee-way sections.

A crown-board is used, instead of the usual quilts, on top of the frames. The crown-board has an opening in the centre to admit a double-exit bee escape, to enable it to be used as a super clearer when required.

The roof is gabled, but constructed in such a way as to permit them being tiered on top of each other.

The method employed of fastening the hive parts together for transportation to the me is extremely simple, but nevertheless most efficient, expeditious, and, moreover, absolutely safe. Two 1/4 in. diameter iron rods, threaded Whitworth bolt thread on one end, and a wing nut fixed stationary to the other end, form the whole outfit for fastening a hive together.

It is accomplished in the following manner: On the front and back of the screen are attached thin, small iron plates, which act as washers. In the centre of each of these plates is a 3/8th in. diameter hole, by which the iron rods are inserted and pushed down between the inside of the hive wall and the end bars of the frames, and through corresponding 3/8th in. holes in the bottom-board, underneath which are attached, with screws, iron plates, 3" x 7/8th" x 3/8th" in size, in each of which is a hole tapped to match the thread on the 1/4 in. rods. The rod, held by the wing nut. is screwed into the plate under the bottom-board, and the screen, shallow-super, brood-chamber arid bottom-board are thereby securely and firmly held together.

Needless to mention, this method of preparing hives for transportation to the moor can be adapted to almost any type of hive. A blacksmith can provide the iron rods and plates for a few pence. As a matter of fact, the plates are not essential; nuts can be attached to the rods under the bottom-board instead. The plates are fitted for convenience sake and the saving of time.

When the bees are taken to the moor. one shallow-super is left on each hive to provide the then necessary clustering space; but when brought back, the brood-chamber by itself furnishes enough room for the bees. Two lengths of rods are therefore required—one set for hives with supers, and a second set for bringing the hives back from the moor without supers.

The actual preparations for conveying bees to the heather are made some time during the day before transportation takes place. The screens and rods are placed in position, but the rod next to the entrance is not screwed tight.

About five o'clock the following morning the bees are first confined into the hives. This is effected by inserting a piece of wood into the aperture of the entrance contracting block. The rod next to the entrance is subsequently screwed tight; the piece of wood confining the bees as well as the entrance contracting block are thereby securely held in position. The hives are then ready for loading.

On reaching the destination on the moor, unloading is proceeded with immediately. When the unloading is over, the iron rods are unscrewed, the alighting-boards placed into position, and then the bees liberated. A few good puffs of smoke are sent in by the entrance on withdrawing the piece of wood confining the bees, and also through the top. The screen is taken off.

The whole operation of loading forty hives, then unloading them on the moor and liberating the bees, occupies about an hour and a half—this, of course, does not include the time spent on the road.

Anyone contemplating transporting bees to the heather might well adopt as his motto "Take no risks." To attempt to shift bees in unsuitable or decrepit hives, or inefficient vehicles, or with unreliable assistance is indeed courting disaster.

Beekeepers are optimists, and it seems, therefore, their fate to learn in the school of experience.

DRIFTING

I believe text-books tell us to arrange hives with entrances facing south-east. This, no doubt, has given rise to what now seems a universal custom of placing hives in straight, symmetrical rows. As a matter of fact, there was no other alternative if entrances must face south-east. However, is it the most satisfactory arrangement from the practical aspect of the question? Indeed not! Anyhow, not on the moor.

If hives are placed in symmetrical order, all facing one direction, then the colonies towards the end of each row, nearest to the moor, possess all the field bees at the close of the season. Drifting on the moor is a great problem. When bees return from the heather laden, they tend to enter the first hive in their line of flight. When heavily laden with nectar, they are freely admitted by any colony. One is then inclined to argue: " What docs it matter, the honey will be obtained nevertheless." Unfortunately, things do not work out that way. It will be found that these abnormally strong stocks never store honey in amounts corresponding to their strength. Furthermore, after the honey-flow, constant lighting takes place, and not infrequently queens are, in consequence, balled and killed. We therefore endeavour to check drifting by every means at our disposal.

The most effective way to avoid drifting is to arrange hives in groups—four hives to a group, and the entrance of each is made to face a different point of the compass. Furthermore, if possible, each group is placed next to a distinguishing mark, as, for instance, a gorse bush, a clump of ferns or a boulder.

There is a further, perhaps the most serious aspect respecting drifting, namely, the dissemination of disease. If there is a diseased colony present, drifting will speedily transmit the malady to other stocks. Indeed, do we not often hear reports of stocks returning from the moor diseased which were perfectly healthy before? I know of a commercial bet-keeper who transports hundreds of hives to a moor a hundred and forty-live miles away rather than place them on a nearby heath, where foul-brood is known to exist.

SHELTER

Shelter from prevailing wind is another important detail conducive to success in the production of heather honey. Where natural shelter is not available, it is well worth the trouble and expense to erect artificial wind-breaks. The lee-side of a hedge forms an ideal place for an apiary.

The inestimable value of shelter was demonstrated to me, many years ago, in a most forcible manner. A short distance from an apiary which was situated in a gully, were twenty-eight hives which, however, we had been compelled to place out on the open moor. One day, when visiting both places, the bees in the gully were found building comb and storing honey quite actively, whereas those in the bleak situation were on the verge of starvation.

The consideration Dartmoor farmers evince respecting the provision of shelter for the bees has always greatly impressed me. These hardy moor-men are most solicitous that the bees should have the advantage of what they call "a looe place."

DARTMOOR

Before proceeding with the subject it will, I feel sure, be not amiss to give a brief description of Dartmoor, for, it must be remembered, much what is said relates mainly to conditions as found on Dartmoor.

It may be recalled that the Celtic name for Devon was Day-fhaint, which means " dark and deep valleys." The south-east approach to Dartmoor is by way of dark and deep valleys. The Dart, the most romantic of rivers, winds its way along in this valley.

The outskirts of the moor are mostly densely wooded; the moor itself, although spoken of as "the forest," is devoid of trees. Dartmoor extends thirty-two miles from south to north, twenty-two miles from east to west, and comprises an area of 130,000 acres. It attains a height of 2.039 feet above sea-level. The forest, except the belt of commons which surround it, is property of the Prince of Wales. The bordering parishes exercise over commons, and to some extent over the forest, rights known as " Venville." Members of venville parishes claim the prerogative to take from forest and commons " anything that may do them good," except green-wood and venison. Tenants in venville pasture their flocks and herds, cut turf and take stone and sand they require. Dartmoor is of volcanic origin, and is mainly composed of granite. The granite, however, is not of uniform quality. Apparently it was not well stirred before being poured out; hence weathers most irregularly. The wreckage, locally termed clitter, thus formed of the tors, in the course of time covers, in some cases, the entire hillsides.

The moor is divided in halves by a road traversing it from east to west. Near its western extremity is situated Princetown Prison. On the northern part of the moor, no road or any human habitations exist.

On the southern half, along the central road, are here and there, surrounded by small plots of cultivated land, a few ancient tenements—the only farms extant on the forest. These farms date back to remote antiquity.

The rest of the moor is a vast, inhospitable wilderness. Long ridges rise behind the other, like waves of the sea. However, the wide, solitary wastes, the rugged, rock-strewn peaks and giant tors impart to Dartmoor a peculiar fascination.

But it is a land of silence—a silence that is awe-inspiring. The faint rustling of cotton-grass and heather, the hum of bees and purling of the moorland streams are the only sounds in this solitude to strike the ear.

Yet in prehistoric time the forest was densely populated. Everywhere are remains of the ancient moor-dwellers. Cyclopean bridges, trackways, stone avenues and hut-circles the ancient Celts built and used can still be seen.

However, it is the honey and pollen-bearing flora of the moor we are foremost interested in.

In spring gorse and broom provide pollen, bluebells and whortleberries nectar. Occasionally gorse flowers a second time simultaneous with the heather.

ERICACEAE

The family of heaths, which botanists call the Ericaceae, include an amazing variety of shrubs and trees. Beekeepers are primarily interested in the genus *Calluna vulgaris*, and in the two common Ericas, *cinerea* and *tetralix* and to a lesser extent in the three rarer species, *ciliaris*, *vagans* and *carnea*.

The Dorset heath, *E. cilians'*, the Cornish heath, *E. vagans*, and the Irish heath, *E. carnea*, are only found in the south of England and Ireland respectively. They are of little value to bees, and we shall therefore not consider them further.

Calluna vulgaris, or ling; *E. cinerea*, or fine-leaved heath; *E. tetralix*, or cross-leaved heath, are found on moors and forests throughout Great Britain.

Erica tetralix, commonly known as bog heather, is usually only found on wet, boggy parts of the moors. It is short in growth and very bushy at the base. The leaves are in fours, formed at each joint of the stems; this fact being set forth in its title " tetralix," meaning four-leaved. It is also called cross-leaved heath, for when viewed from above, the four leaves assume the form of a cross. It blooms in July. The flowers are most gracefully formed, and the wax-like, rosy-hued bells are always borne at the top of the spikes, in drooping little clusters of close umbels, all facing in one direction.

Bog heath, though not as showy as bell heather, is undoubtedly the most charming of the two. It is not abundant on Dartmoor, and generally grows only to a height of a few inches. I know of only one spot where it develops to perfection. *E. tetralix* yields pollen and nectar.

Erica cinerea, commonly called bell heather, forms a bushy growth. Its branches spring mostly separate from the base, and grow to a height of about twelve inches. The leaves are sharply pointed, and grow in whorls around the stems. The flowers are a rich, reddish purple, produced on upright spikes in dense terminal racemes one above another, and are bell-shaped in form. Bell heather is in full bloom about mid-July, but it can still be found in flower here and there throughout the autumn.

E. cinerea flourishes mostly on the foot-hills and outskirts of Dartmoor. It does not thrive on the higher regions of the moor. Bell heather is the main source of nectar on the low-lying moors of southern England. On Dartmoor, on the contrary, I have known it to yield heavily only one season, in 1920. The honey derived from this source is usually a lovely crimson-red in colour, but in some districts is as dark as treacle. It is fair in flavour, but lacks body, and granulates with a course grain.

Calluna vulgaris, or ling, whilst not so attractive as the Ericas, is nevertheless of foremost economic value. It is from the ling that the world-famed, the true heather honey is derived.

The ling forms a rather straggly shrub, usually about a foot in height. Its branches are tough and more woody than in the other two species. The leaves, borne on close masses on the side shoots, are very small, and, moreover, are covered with knobby-hairs. The flowers vary in colour from a deep purple to a very pale pink, and occasionally are found pure white.

The ling is in flower from July 25th to September 20th in normal seasons, but secretes nectar generally only from mid-August until September 5th, the period when it is in full bloom. The honey varies in colour from a light amber to red-brown, has a jelly-like consistency, a bitter-sweet flavour, and an all-pervading fragrance.

A complexity of factors, of which as yet very little is known definitely, affect the secretion, flavour, colour, viscosity, and, to some extent, aroma of heather honey.

SUBSOIL

The mere presence of an abundance of bloom does not denote that nectar will be forthcoming. Very little honey is derived from ling, for instance, on the moors around Aldershot, the New Forest and in Dorsetshire, although there is a wealth of bloom, in fact far more of it than anywhere on Dartmoor. Whilst a lime-free surface soil is essential for the well-being of heather, the absence of nectar is accounted for by the particular subsoil of the southern moors. I believe it is generally maintained that no nectar is secreted on sandy or chalky subsoil, and that ling yields most freely, and honey of prime quality, on granite or ironstone —which our own experience seems to corroborate. Whereas almost the whole of Dartmoor is granite, the heather is singularly confined to the area where tin-streaming was in progress in centuries gone by. Is the presence of iron in the tin-bearing ore the cause of this curious phenomenon?

SWALING

Another condition affecting the secretion of nectar is the formation of growth, or the age of the plant. When ling is permitted to grow on for years, without any interference, it forms rank, woody growth. Although it will then still flower, the nectar obtained therefrom is quantitatively less, and also considered qualitatively inferior.

The burning-off of heather, or " swaling," as it is termed by moorfolk, is therefore a blessing in disguise to beekeepers. This we never fully appreciated until the past dry summer. The parts of the moor which were burnt over two or three years ago produced this season a veritable mass of bloom, whereas the old, straggly heather, acres and acres of it, hardly formed any bloom. A Staffordshire beekeeper reported the same occurrence on Cannock Chase moors this season.

Subsequent to a conflagration, two or three years have to elapse before the heather comes into full bloom again.

ALTITUDE

Originally, our apiaries were situated on the southern out-skirts of Dartmoor, at elevations of approximately nine hundred feet above sea-level. The locations were considered ideal for the production of heather honey. However, a few years later an apiary was established at an altitude of 1,500 ft. The difference in the quantity and quality of the honey obtained on the higher moor was most remarkable. Now nearly all our apiaries are located around the highest points, approachable by road, of the southern half of Dartmoor. Last year we secured about 32 Ib. more honey from colonies at elevations of 1,500 ft. compared to the stocks still on the lower ranges of the moor. As conditions were identical in all localities, where the apiaries are situated, altitude, in this case, must mainly account for the difference in the yield. Still there is no denying the fact that heather honey is obtained at elevations below 800 ft. But to get heather honey of supreme quality, a high altitude seems essential.

CLIMATIC CONDITIONS

The most outstanding characteristic of ling is its ability of yielding in minimum temperatures, when no nectar could reason-ably be expected of any other flowers. Instances are on record when it actually secreted heavily subsequent to a severe hoar frost. I remember one season, 1923, when the maxima never exceeded 67 degrees throughout the duration of the flow. We nevertheless obtained a crop which in quantity, and especially in quality, left little to desire. Notwithstanding, nectar is secreted most liberally with night temperatures of not less than 42 degrees, and day temperatures fluctuating between 70-78 degrees. But, so I am led to conclude, a humid atmosphere, with a drift of air from a southerly direction, is as essential for a heavy flow as any other factor. With a current of air from the northeast or north, there may be every other condition present conducive to a flow, but no nectar will be forthcoming. The ideal close, sultry weather seems invariably of short duration at the time the heather is in bloom. After three or four perfect days for nectar secretion, thundery weather develops, which generally denotes the conclusion of the honey-flow that season.

DURATION OF HONEY-FLOWS

Seldom or hardly ever is a heather honey-flow protracted. In most seasons it lasts but a few days. In 1917 heather honey was gathered only during a couple of hours one afternoon. The most protracted flow I remember, extended over a period of twenty-six days without any cessation. Although nectar is secreted on the moor during comparatively brief spells, this is counterbalanced by the fact that no other honey plant in the British Isles yields as profusely when conditions are favourable. Instances are on record where stocks of average strength made gains of 10 lb. in the space of a few hours. The yield from August 25th to the 28th last year was undoubtedly the most phenomenal flow we have ever witnessed.

In normal seasons, no heather honey seems ever to be gathered either before mid-August or after September loth. So on or about September 5th, all the supers are placed on bee escapes. There-after we endeavour to lose no time in getting the hives back from the moor, to permit wintering preparations to be completed by October 1st.

FEEDING

This brings me to the much debated question of the suitability of heather honey as a winter food for bees.

Many experienced heather men declare it absolutely detrimental, whilst others, on the contrary, hold heather honey to be an excellent winter food. Our own experience in this matter leaves no doubt that heather honey cannot, year after year, be relied upon to carry bees safely through winter. We therefore have made it a practice to feed each colony about 15 Ib. of syrup, regardless of the amount of stores they may have before closing down for winter. Ever since, our winter losses are negligible.

The syrup fed is composed of sugar and water only; nothing else is added. The proportions are: 7½lb. water to 10 Ib. sugar. The syrup is prepared by the cold process, that is, the sugar is merely dissolved in cold water.

Our tank was specially erected to facilitate preparing syrup by the cold process. The correct quantity of cold water is allowed to flow into the tank, then the sugar added, and an occasional stirring to keep the sugar in suspension is all that is required to dissolve it. A ton of sugar takes about two hours to convert into syrup.

The tank is lined with glazed tiles, with the object of avoiding every possible danger of contamination, as would be the case with a metallic container. We are, moreover, thus enabled to prepare the syrup long in advance at our entire convenience.

EXTRACTING

Whilst the work of bringing back the hives from the moor, and the feeding and wintering are in progress, the extracting of the heather honey is also proceeded with. Immediately the crop is off the hives we endeavour to extract it without delay.

Honey derived from bell heather can be extracted by means of centrifugal force, in fact it leaves the combs more readily than flower honey. The true heather honey—the honey of jelly-like consistency—no amount of centrifugal force can possibly dislodge from the comb, except the contents of each cell is first loosened and then extracted before the honey re-assumes the gelatinous state. This, in fact, is the principle involved in the heather honey loosening machine, first placed on the market in 1906. But as bees build comb irregularly, it is next to impossible .to construct a machine which will effectively loosen the contents of each cell of a comb. Moreover, even after treatment with a heather honey loosener, genuine ling honey will not extract as clean as flower honey, and unless the extracted combs can be given back to the bees to be cleaned before cold weather sets in, the remaining honey will deteriorate, and thereby affect the crop subsequently stored in them. Also, in the process of treating heather honey, the needles of the honey loosener unavoidably break down some cell-walls, which in extracting axe bound to get into the honey. Due to the peculiar consistency of heather honey, it is practically impossible to free it of the particles of wax subsequently. There is, to my knowledge, no satisfactory means by which ling honey can be strained.

Where heather honey in run form is produced, a press of some kind is essential. If only a small quantity of surplus has to be dealt with a hand squeezer, made of two pieces of wood each two feet in length, and three inches in width by an inch in thickness, hinged together at one end, will answer the purpose. The honey-comb is cut out of the frame, tied in cheese-straining cloth, and the bag hung up, then the comb crushed with the hand squeezer, and thereby the honey liberated from the wax. We ourselves used an appliance of this kind many years ago. However, where a large crop has to be dealt with, this method is too wasteful and slow; a specially constructed honey press is then required.

A press must be substantially constructed to extract honey efficiently. Very considerable pressure is demanded to get honey satisfactorily out of comb. We have used no less than six different types of presses. Eventually, as there is no press on the market for dealing with large crops efficiently and expeditiously, we were compelled to design and construct one of our own.

To operate the machine, the pressing-board is hrst detached from the beam, and pushed back out of the way on the trolley. A sheet of cheese-straining cloth, six feet square, is next spread over the grid container. The combs of heather honey are then cut from their frames and laid side by side five high on top of each other inside the press container, which admits fifty shallow-combs at one pressing. When full, the overlapping straining cloth is folded over the top of the combs, the pressing-board pulled forward into position and attached to the beam; the beam, with the pressing-board suspended on it, is then slightly raised, to permit the trolley to be pushed behind the press. The motor is then stopped and switched into reverse, when slowly but surely the pressing-board is forced down on the honey-combs. Immediately the motor indicates stress, the low gear is engaged, which transmits twelve revolutions to the worm-drive, and develops a pressure of over a hundred tons to the square inch. An idea can be formed of the efficiency of the machine by the fragment of a sheet of wax taken from the press. From the six inches of combs a sheet of nearly solid wax, 3/8th in. in thickness, is all that remains inside the straining cloth. The marks of the wire screen, impressed on the wax, are plainly visible. The cheese straining cloth is, subsequent to each pressing, rinsed in clean water to prevent the bits of wax adhering to it from getting into the honey already extracted.

An almost insuperable difficulty, connected with every type of honey press we used, was to find a cheese-straining cloth which would withstand the enormous stress it had to be subjected to in pressing honey. The straining cloth supplied by appliance dealers was, after two or three pressings, torn beyond repair. A year ago we were eventually successful in procuring a cheese-straining cloth of the quality required. One sheet of the new straining cloth enabled us to do no less than seventy-five pressings before it had finally to be discarded. note.—The combs are slightly warmed before being pressed

As already stated, the honey, after it is extracted, collects in a tank at the rear of the press. From there it is delivered, by a specially designed power-driven rotary pump, into the storage vats on the second floor.

Whilst seasons of plenty and scarcity do not come in periods of seven years, nevertheless, to assure customers a continuous supply it was found imperative to provide for seasons of failure, which, especially in heather honey production, greatly predominate. With this object in view special storage vats were built.

There are eleven tanks, totalling a storage capacity of nearly thirty tons. The internal dimensions of each tank are 7' x 3' x 3'. They are lined with tinned steel plate, made to our requirements. The lids, on account of condensation, are covered on the underside with aluminium. Between the lids and the top of the tanks is a rubber tape which, when the lid is bolted down, seals the tanks hermetically. The honey can therefore be kept indefinitely, without any deterioration, in these tanks.

FILLING MACHINE

We use an electrically operated bottle-filler. This filling machine enables a tank full of honey to be emptied into I lb. containers in the space of three hours, or fills on an average 2,000 cartons in sixty minutes. Each container is filled exact weight, without any drip.

In each of the eleven tanks is installed a coil, composed of 125 ft. of I in. bore tinned copper tubing. The coils are connected to a gas-heated, thermostatically controlled boiler. The temperature of the water circulating in the coils can be regulated to a nicety. When the coils are empty, they can be detached and bodily lifted out of the tanks for cleaning. The time required to liquefy a tank full of solid, granulated clover honey, two and a half tons, is eighteen to twenty-four hours.

This brings me to the question of granulation of heather honey, or, to be more precise, granulation in heather honey. For, I believe, it is generally admitted that pure ling honey never granulates, which our own experience seems to confirm. In 1923 no heather honey was gathered on Dartmoor until September 8th, and then throughout the duration of the flow, the maximum temperature was so low that, even if there had been other flowers, no honey would have been secreted by them. In consequence, the crop that year was probably pure ling honey. Anyhow, it never manifested the slightest sign of granulation. Occasionally the honey we obtain granulates to a consistency of soft butter, but the typical Dartmoor heather honey stays liquid; crystals are formed only here and there, kept suspended in the honey. This kind of granulation is, no doubt, accounted for by a slight admixture of honey derived from bell heather.

When for any reason heat has to be applied to heather honey, the utmost care has to be exercised. In no case must the temperature of the honey exceed 130 degrees, or be kept at this temperature for any length of time. There is no other honey of which the flavour, aroma and consistency is so easily ruined by the application of heat. Heather honey swells considerably when heated, and allowance must therefore be made for the expansion which takes place.

HEATHER HONEY

We have in our possession a collection of samples of heather honey derived from all over the British Isles. Hardly two samples are alike regarding colour, flavour or granulation, and, although considered pure heather honey, some flow exactly as ordinary flower honey does. Apparently any honey obtained on or near a moor is designated " heather honey." However, there is a decided, unmistakable difference between the true heather honey derived from the ling, and bell heather honey, or the numerous blends. Ling honey is distinguishable from other honeys by a simple test. If, on inverting a jar of liquid honey, the contents do not flow, then it certainly is heather honey. I do not mean to imply that a honey which does not flow is 100 per cent, pure, but that the true heather honey predominates.

Although Ericas are commonly spoken of as heather, they are, to be precise, heaths; the ling, heather. Heaths and heather belong to the same family, but of the ling only one species exists, whereas of the genus Erica there are numerous species, five of which are indigenous in the British Isles. Moreover, the true heather honey possesses a flavour, aroma and consistency absolutely unlike any other honey. That from the heaths has not the faintest resemblance to it, excepting colour.

The Ministry of Agriculture has recently issued regulations whereby heather honey is now placed under the National Mark. This undoubtedly is a great step forward in bringing heather honey into its rightful position.

All our heather honey is marketed in a special carton.

After the meeting Bro. Adam was subjected to the usual bombardment of questions, which he answered with great courtesy.

A very hearty vote of thanks was passed, but the most complimentary token of regard to his great work in making beekeeping a real business proposition was the exceptional gathering of nearly three hundred beekeepers from a large area of the north.

HEATHER HONEY
by
COLIN WEIGHTMAN

"Wild blossoms of the moorland, ye are very dear to me;
Ye lure my dreaming memory as clover does the bee;
Ye bring back all my childhood loved, when freedom, joy, and health,
Had never thought of wearing chains to fetter fame and wealth."
Eliza Cook

Former member of MAFF's Bee Disease Advisory Committee & Bee Husbandry Committee and Honorary Member British Beekeepers Association.

1st Published in the Beekeeping in a Nutshell series by Northern Bee Books

© Colin Weightman

INTRODUCTION

We are dealing with areas in the British Isles where the ling heather CALLUNA vulgaris is found and to a lesser extent the bell heathers ERICAS cinerea & tetralix and Scottish beekeepers produce a pleasing run honey from the bell heather - usually in July - which can be readily extracted. For, the beekeeper, the best heather moors are the well managed grouse moors,where, the old ling is burnt on a regular basis to encourage new growth. And, here, the good will of Land Owners, Farmers and Gamekeepers must be sought and their requirements respected at all times. It is an unfortunate fact that many members of the public demand that they should have unrestricted access to open moorland and hill often causing havoc among wild life and nesting birds. Beekeepers, too, often in their early days unwittingly fall into this trap. Moving their bee colonies on to the moors in late July and August and setting the hives down 'willy nilly' without prior consultation with anyone. Hives of bees from which supers of blossom honey have been recently removed house bees which can be unusually vindictive - at the sudden loss of their stores - are sometimes set down behind walls, close to footpaths, bridle paths and shooting butts: causing annoyance to walkers, pony treckers and shooting parties and their beaters, Before setting hives down anywhere - prior arrangement regarding permission, rent and siting, must be obtained from the parties concerned. Failure to do so can sometimes lead to the confiscation and loss of hives.

A heather stance must be chosen with care - often a gully, or sheltered valley, can be found where the hives can be set down on their own. Make sure the spot will not flood as there have been many occasions when hives have been partly submerged and even washed away after torrential downpours on the moorland tops. Shelter is of the utmost importance and the bees should be able to fly out up the hill and come down hill loaded. Often, dark clouds of homecoming bees can be seen skimming the wall tops as they return to the hives after battling against strong winds on the open moor. Avoid communal stances, where, anything up to 100 stocks of bees are set down together, - often in straight rows - as there is a tendency for the bees to drift. A group of hives, with the entrances facing in different directions, is a better arrangement altogether. In small scale operations a simple hive stand - carrying - two hives - which can be carried on a pickup when moving bees is a useful additional piece of equipment to enable the hives to be kept off the ground, But, many stocks taken to the heather are set down on the ground - and levelled up with small pieces of stone. Unless a temporary alighting board is placed in front of the hive: growing heather or bracken may soon restrict hive entrances - compelling the returning foragers to run down the hive fronts to gain entry. Entrance blocks reducing hive entrances to around 12 inches in width and 3/4 inch high should always be in use to discourage slugs and rodents from gaining entry. In hot summers Adders are sometimes found under the hives when they are placed directly on the ground and rubber boots are best worn to avoid snake bites, or, the bees attacking the ankles.

Wear industrial or strong leather gloves when lifting hives off the ground.

It is another unfortunate fact of human nature that whenever a beekeeper finds a stance, where over the yesars bees do well, other beekeepers will endeavour to take their stocks there too - and these moorland apiaries become eventually over stocked with bee colonies.

Twenty colonies to a stance - not far apart - will, if the colonies have been properly prepared: result in consistent performance - usually a super of sealed heather, comb honey, a hive, as against a lot of unsealed honey, where too many colonies are set down together. Some beekeepers erect permanent stands on the moors to carry the hives and use a spirit level to ensure that the combs hang correctly in the supers. For really choice combs of heather honey - full sheets of medium - thickness worker brood foundation (unwired) should be used. However, many heather going beekeepers use 'starters' only in the supers - cutting a sheet of shallow worker brood foundation into three strips - in such cases the top part of the comb is usually drawn out with the attractive flat matt capping of worker cells while the rest of the comb has drone cells: which some customers prefer. The practice of using extra - thin foundation should be discouraged - as all too often this collapses in really strong colonies of bees and many fine combs are spoilt each year. Only unwired foundation is used in the supers for cut comb honey and pressed heather honey. When, hives are placed on stands on the moors, occasionally during a really heavy nectar flow -and excessive crowding - the bees will come out of their hives and build wild comb which they fill with honey under the floorboards. This happened in 1911. 1949, 1955, 1969 1972 and 1981. Nineteen Forty nine had, what was probably the earliest, and heaviest, nectar flow from the ling on record. Heather honey was being stored in the combs by July 20th, and bees being worked on a small brood chamber of 8 - 10 B.S. combs, filled and sealed a super a week: and this went on for five weeks. In late seasons it is an advantage to use drawn comb in the supers - combs drawn out earlier on the Oil Seed Rape can be extracted - and then given back to the bees above clearer boards for them to clean, and if sprayed with warm water they will make a very good job of it, and you will be left with some fine dry drawn out combs from which all trace of the OSR honey has gone.

There must be no trace of OSR honey in the hives when you take them to the heather: otherwise, it will ruin your crop of heather comb honey as early crystallisation sets in. Outside combs of stores containing 'set' OSR honey must be removed, too, from the brood chambers and replaced with brood combs of heather honey - if you have them - from the season before. It is a sound investment to get some brood combs filled with heather honey when the bees are on the moors, as, such combs, are wonderful for feeding purposes the following spring and the colonies are given a real boost. It is believed that by providing your heather going colonies with combs of heather honey - from the year before - this will get the bees out foraging days ahead of the colonies not so provided for.

Just as the late Brother Adam was convinced that colonies taken to the moor should always be headed by queens - in their second year - and that the excitement of the move actually stimulated egg laying,

While, most heather going beekeepers use queen excluders on the moors, for starters and ekes will result in a lot of drone comb, and queens are particularly attracted to laying in the larger drone cells, even late in the season, if they are available: resulting in many spoilt combs which should have held honey. But, there are occasions, particularly in late seasons, or, when the nights are cold and the bees tend to move out of the supers altogether - when queen-excluders can be dispensed with and removed - if already on the hives. Experienced beekeepers often obtain some combs of heather honey this way - when other beekeepers get nothing in the supers.

Traditionally, heather comb honey was produced in sections on the moors and the small racks holding no more then 18 sections fitted inside an empty brood chamber - used as a super and was warmly packed with at least three folded hessian sacks: as warmth necessary for comb building and sealing, had to be encouraged by every possible means. Section racks, holding up to 32 sections, which covered the entire brood chamber as a super, were, as a general rule,useless on the moors: and many beekeepers were discouraged for good, when trying to work with them. A wide shallow frame carrying 3 sections was sometimes used and in recent times ROSS ROUND combs have been tried by some. But the simplicity of cut comb heather honey produced in shallow frames - Manley and Hoffman

- outweighs them all. The narrower spacing of the latter is popular where families buy a few complete combs at a time and return the empty frames to the beekeeper the following spring.

HIVES

National and Smith hives are ideal for heather work as the small brood chambers -of both - ensures, that having been reduced from two brood chambers to a single brood chamber at the beginning of July - you have an enormous force of foraging bees. As the brood emerges the bees store honey in the brood combs and this brood chamber is removed altogether at the end of the month - with the aid of a clearer board if all the brood has hatched. If there is still sealed brood in some of the combs then the bees must be shaken or, brushed off the combs with a goose wing feather, into the bottom brood chamber and the combs without bees used to 'boost' nucleus or, smaller colonies. The bottom brood chamber will be immensely crowded and a super of shallow combs with the frames fitted, if possible with full sheets of medium thickness worker base foundation unwired, or, with starters of the same, or, drawn out combs if you have them, are given to the colony above a queen excluder. The inner - cover board is then replaced - with ideally some form of packing or insulation immediately above. One super is enough to start with. The mistake so often made is to provide too much room at the heather. Two supers are often provided and invariably there are a number of unsealed combs in the second. If you are working for choice cut - comb heather honey it is much better to have as many combs as possible sealed. For those beekeepers 'geared up' with moisture extraction facilities unsealed heather honey no longer presents a problem - and they are quite happy to get as much heather honey as possible - even, if it is unsealed. The brood chambers of blossom honey removed before going to the heather are piled up on hive stands - with clearer boards between each - and a hive roof on top: to be returned to the bees for over - wintering. Wrap in strong plastic sheeting too to keep wasps out. When reducing double brood chamber colonies to one brood chamber the problem of crowding all the bees into a smaller area must be tackled. Two supers - the top one containing drawn comb -previously cleaned by the bees and dry. While the super immediately above the queen excluder and the brood nest contains shallow frames fitted with unwired medium worker brood foundation, or, starters of the same. These, are topped by a screen board - with a deep rim on the bottom part - this will usually accommodate the large force of bees - when the bottom entrance to the hive is completely closed with an entrance block or strip of foam. Many experienced heather - going beekeepers leave the entrance open to allow the bees to cluster up the front of the hive - leaving the entrance block with its 12 inch aperture in place. The beekeeper must have considerable confidence to tackle moving bees in this way. Bee veil, and suit, rubber boots (Wellingtons) strong leather or industrial gloves, to prevent tearing hands on projecting metal parts, namely, hive tops, excluders, broken hive staples which have at various times been used to attach floorboards to brood chambers along with functional smokers; are all basic requirements. It is an advantage to have two strong hardwood laths screwed to the bottom of each floorboard - to provide additional strength and to facilitate lifting of hives.

The use of strapping is the current popular means of securing hive parts but, often beekeepers complement this, by securing the hive floorboard to the brood chamber with hive staples at each corner. Hive entrances are best closed while doing this to prevent bees pouring out to sting the operator: opening the entrances immediately afterwards. As, invariably, when loading hives manually and pushing them along a floor, something will come apart. Carry something like Blue tack and small pieces of foam rubber, to plug holes, etc from which bees can escape. Buckfast Abbey carried toilet tissue - for this purpose - when moving bees to the heather. In heather districts some beekeepers attach hinged floorboards to their hives with ventilation holes covered with strong perforated zinc or wiremesh. The Scottish firm STEELE & BRODIE listed such a floorboard in their catalogue for years - with a thumbscrew permanently attached below - to aid easy closing. Such hives should always be set on stands, rather than on the ground, as growing heather and bracken, can, on occasion, close the entrance altogether unless a small stone or piece of wood has been placed in position to prevent this.

There, is an equally effective-system of colony management for the heather: for those who prefer to run their bees in small, single brood chamber, hives on 10 BS combs. Ideally, suited for those working bees on their own, where the lifting of heavy hives can be a problem - and the removal and manipulation of several brood chambers - with the concentration of a large foraging force of bees into a single brood chamber: off putting, to many.

In late April or early May, where colonies have over-wintered well and are expanding beyond expectations on the nectar flow of the Oil Seed Rape. **Do not super;** and the congestion, thus created, will inevitably compel the bees to 'put up' a few choice queen cells. In districts where there is no nectar flow from the Oil Seed Rape these conditions of prosperity can be brought about by the heavy feeding of sugar syrup. When, these conditions are met, a good 5 comb Nucleus colony is made up in the empty brood chamber, of a similar type of hive, alongside. Making sure that the old queen is left in the parent colony, where, the combs removed, are replaced with drawn out combs - if available - on the outsides of the 5 remaining combs. Otherwise 5 frames fitted with sheets of wired worker base foundation are utilised - again , on the outsides of the 5 remaining combs, which should of course be in the centre of the brood chamber.

This, Nucleus,has 3 combs of emerging brood - densely covered with bees - with the queen cells too, and great care must be taken not to shake, or, jar these particular combs and then there are 2 combs of stores on the outsides of the combs of brood: followed by a dummy board on each side. It is essential that the hive containing the Nucleus colony has a small entrance - which is completely closed with tightly packed grass for several days - which, as it dries out -

the bees will remove. No bees must escape to return to the parent colony alongside - until the bees in the Nucleus eat their own way out. Once, the bees achieve this, and begin working normally from the small entrance, the surviving young queen should soon mate, and a check 14 days later should establish this. By the end of May it should be possible to boost the Nucleus colony with a comb of emerging brood from the parent colony alongside and continuing at fortnightly intervals throughout June: until the full complement of 10 BS is made up. By mid-July the Nucleus colony - with the young queen - should be packed with hatching bees and in an ideal condition to be taken to the heather - and at this stage it is provided with a super. On a warm afternoon -when there is a nectar flow in progress - move the parent colony away on to another stand in the apiary. So, the returning foragers will further boost the Nucleus colony built up during the summer, Really 'topping' heather going colonies are obtained this way, There, can be uniting -with newspaper upon return from the moors - if the object is to keep the number of honey producing colonies the same in the apiary - while maintaining a high level of production. The move to the moors should always be made at break of day - loading up to be away by 5 a.m. -reaching the moors before the powerful rays of the sun can be felt - as many powerful colonies of bees are lost over the years from overheating and suffocation. There is no more distressing sight than to lose a top colony of bees this way - which usually involves the collapse of the combs and honey pouring from the hive entrance. Unless it is a cool damp evening and you know exactly where you are going to, and you are not going to get stuck: moving bees at night can be fraught with difficulties - as during the warm evenings of late July and early August - the bees are often still returning to their hives as darkness falls and many actually stay out all night on flowers and return the following morning when the hives have gone much to their distress. If you have some colonies still left at home these 'lost' foragers will usually join them.

A

Colony on single small brood chamber holding 9 BS combs and dummy board with super of 8 Manley shallow frames at the heather. Note brood combs being filled with stores for winter.

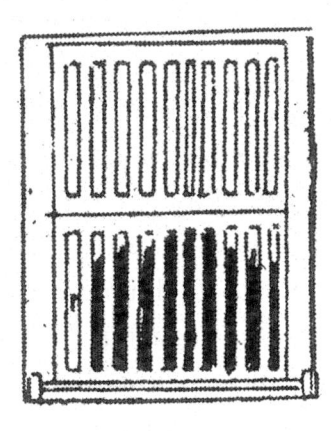

B

The same colony in mid-April of the following year with combs almost all filled with brood being provided with second brood chamber for the Oil Seed Rape with the frames fitted with wired worker base foundation.

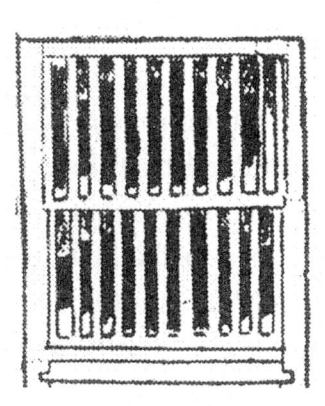

C

Early June when the second brood chamber - like the first - is filled with brood.

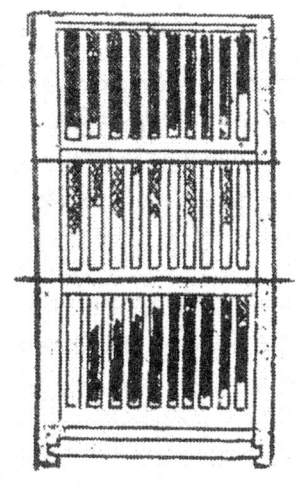

D

End of June. Second brood is raised above a super(s) of empty combs to the top of the hive with a queen excluder between them and the bottom brood chamber

Grass, such as lawn mowings along with damp moss, is excellent for dosing hive entrances, if the move - to and from the moor - is only a short one as it has the additional advantage of allowing the bees to eat their way out of the hive should the beekeeper overlook this. Unfortunately this happens somewhere in the country, every year. Having arrived on the moor safely with the bees and got the hives onto their stands - a feeling of satisfaction prevails - the possibility of a record crop of heather honey is within reach. Lulled into a false sense of well-being, the beekeeper and helpers set out for home: without double-checking each hive to ensure that the bees in every one can get out. It is worth returning to the heather stance later in the day to ensure that all is well.

The small single brood chambers of National and Smith hives are ideal for heather work ensuring that much of the honey goes into the single super and is sealed, and by the end of August the bees store honey in the brood combs - as the brood emerges - and bee colonies taken to the heather moors, are usually well provisioned for the winter, and as experienced beekeepers know the high protein content of this honey, ensures that these colonies will have more 'zip' -to them than the colonies that have stayed at home and been overwintered on blossom honey, - a large part of which is often crystallised Oil Seed Rape honey. The National hive - improved by the late Arthur Abbot of Mountain Grey Apiaries, Brough York's, with its splendid brood chamber and super handling features: allow these to be carried easily by beekeepers on their own. A great improvement on the cups' scooped out of the sides of hives assembled from four pieces of wood. With such hives some beekeepers screw a length of wood on each side of the brood chamber and super to facilitate lifting. The Smith hive is often described as a small Langstroth. Beekeepers, such as Athole Kirkwood, have had success with the standard Langstroth hive on the moors, while, in North Yorkshire John Whent operates a thousand or more colonies of bees, working with standard Langstroth equipment and using brood chambers as supers on the moors. With such a large comb area there is often much unsealed heather honey - but with modern moisture extracting equipment - the moisture content of the honey can be reduced down to an acceptable 20% and unsealed heather honey is now no longer the problem it once was. Many small-scale beekeepers use simple moisture extraction devices in their honey stores. Spare bedrooms, too, with central heating, are sometimes used to store heather honey in the supers. The Commercial hive with its 16" x 10" frame and National and Smith hives taking the 14" x 12" frame are used by other beekeepers, with some measure of success at the heather. While, others work with the even larger Dadant. These larger hives are extremely heavy when filled with heather honey and the crops from simpler smaller hives can be equal and often better at the heather. For successful over-wintering, the honey from the Ling must be sealed and the bee colonies sited so the hives catch the mid-day sun, to encourage the bees to take cleansing flights in mid- winter. A top entrance to the hive can be an advantage too. All too often there can be much unsealed heather honey in the combs and unless such colonies are fed heavily with thick warm sugar syrup, there will be problems galore from fermentation. Honey from the Ling is notorious for absorbing moisture and, if left in the unsealed state on the hives will soon be frothing in the combs, which is lethal to the bees. I have on a number of occasions visited moorland apiaries at the request of beekeepers where heather honey, much of it unsealed - had been left on the hives to find brown excreta running from hive entrances and this unpleasant smell will always stay with you. In severe winters when the bees have been confined to their hives for weeks on end the first cleansing flight will be remembered for the pungent smell of heather honey in the apiary, as the bees on the wing void their faeces.

When supers have been removed and hefting of .the hives with the roofs off reveals that they feel light in weight and have little reserves of stores in the brood chambers. Then, such colonies must be provided with slabs of fondant placed immediately above the bees - and, then, checks are made throughout the winter as the bees consume this.

BEST BEES

Strains of the north European dark bee (Apis mellifera mellifera) adapted to the district, give over a period of years, the best performance at the heather. Many of the dark bees found in the British Isles stem from the extensive imports of Dutch bees, Ligurians from Northern Italy, and French, Blacks, which the Scottish firm of Steele & Brodie made available to British beekeepers from their supplier William Wilson. These LE GATINAIS Bees from Grigneville. Loiret, and Faronville, France were, apart from their uncertain temperament - highly thought of amongst comb honey producers in this country: as the firm's 1927 advert shows. "As recommended by J.M.Ellis of Gretna Green whose two stocks produced 240 finished sections which sold for £20". Both, the late Brother Adam and Ted Humphreys recalled that for heather honey production these bees had no equal. But, on a number of occasions these gentlemen had to retreat from the bees fiery onslaughts. Brother Adam himself, standing half submerged in the mill race which meanders through the Abbey grounds. Thornes, too, had their own supplier. Like many other beekeepers I have tried light coloured American and New Zealand bees over a period of 50 years. The extreme docility of these bees is their main claim to fame but for serious heather work they should be avoided. They, will certainly fill supers of heather honey in their first season,but invariably the colonies collapse with Acarine infestation and Nosema during the winter months and following spring. The crosses, from the colonies that do survive, are, as as a general rule, unpleasant bees to work with as Woodbury observed in the 1850's when he first introduced Ligurian bees into Devon. Charlton, who started the Northumberland BKA in 1888, favoured the Ligurian bee for out-crossing as many colonies of the local dark bee had serious defects of the brood, which the introduction of the Ligurian, corrected.

William Herrod - Hempsall, Brother Adam, Manley and Gale all enthused, at various times, about the virtures of the yellow bee when they were obliged to restock following the enormous losses to the honey bee population of this country, up to, and following the first World War. It is now thought that this was brought about by a combination of factors: including the mite Acarapis woodii - along with viruses - and poor beekeeping practice.

Following the adoption of the movable comb hive - which allowed beekeepers to remove almost all the honey from the bees - replacing it with sugar syrup and candy Manley gave beekeepers a clear warning of the folly of this in his book BEEKEEPING IN BRITAIN (1948) page 367. This, along with his remarks about the brood defects of bees, should be carefully considered today. William Herrod - Hempsall, after losing the dark bees which he so much loved, worked with A. I. Root's Red Clover strain from the USA and developed a strain of yellow banded bee, which, surprisingly, could be accommodated on 10 B.S. combs. But, he went on to encounter serious over-wintering problems which he attributed to Nosema.

Traditional heather going beekeeping in many parts of the country is now intrinsically tied up with coping with winter sown Oil Seed Rape which flowers from April through to June and then the spring sown varieties which flower in mid-June and July, a small brood chamber of 10 B.S. combs, use of a queen excluder and lack of adequate supering results in a spate of swarming from mid-April onwards. Often, swarms come off without queen cells being started in the hive. A new generation of beekeeper has appeared to take advantage of the situation, and they collect all the swarms they can, and set them up in hives: and, if prudent, treating them for mites. Hived, initially, on 5 B.S,frames fitted with sheets of wired worker base foundation and dummy boards on the outsides of the frames and some lose sacking in the outside space to prevent the bees from building wild comb, along with a feeder, and some simple packing to conserve heat above the bees. New, additional frames are added as the original complement are drawn out. By the end of July these are usually 'topping' stocks to go to the moor on a single brood chamber and one super.

PROBLEMS ON THE MOORS

There are seasons of complete failure on the moors such as 1912, 1946, 1954 and 1985 when, many bee colonies taken to the moors, were lost from starvation. I well recall going round the stances of many northern beekeepers during August 1946 and August 1954 and finding the ground in front of the hives carpeted with crawling dying bees. Milk churns filled with sugar syrup were taken to the moors and where ever possible the crawling bees were swept up on to shovels and dumped into the tops of nearby hives then lightly sprayed with syrup. After, an hour or so, when there was some response from the bees, and they were gently humming - the old type of round feeders were put on every hive. The feeders were replenished every other day and eventually among those colonies that had not died out - a small amount of heather honey was stored in the brood combs and with further heavy feeding of the colonies upon their return home some of these stocks of bees managed to survive the dreadful winter which set in around January 20th 1947 and continued until April of that year. But, honey again poured into the hives in August and September 1947.

It would appear that hours of sunshine play an important part in the equation when the colonies are on the moors. Similarly, after the dreadful summer of 1954, the bees stored a small amount of heather honey in September of that year and then, virtually, no more honey was taken into the hives until July 1955, when, an altogether fantastic nectar flow went on and on into September. Again, hours of sunshine, played their part in this. Sometimes, during a heavy nectar flow at the heather, honey / nectar will be deposited in cells containing eggs - submerging them completely. In some years the Heather Beetle LOCHMOEA suturalis becomes a nuisance. Dr Guy Morison described the activities of the beetle in 1936 . A swarm of beetles had been seen to land on the waters of Loch Awe in Argyllshire and were speedily devoured by the trout as they struggled on the surface. Their habit is to take wing in swarms in Spring and travel wherever the wind takes them - which may be up to two miles and cover hundreds of acres. In Britain, and particularly in Scotland in 1935, severe damage by the heather beetle was wide - spread, the West and South-West areas appeared to suffer most. Heather of any age is liable to attack: but whereas young vigorous heather up to eight or ten years is seldom killed, old heather of twenty years or more often succumbs to the attack of the beetle, and on moors where severe damage occurs most of the heather is very old. During the 1970's the heather moors of the northern Pennines - between Blanchland and Stanhope - where, incidently, there are some fine stands of Bell heather (Erica cinerea) were attacked by the beetle on several occasions.

REMOVAL OF THE CROP

Early in September clearer boards are put on the hives during late afternoons, boards, which hold several porter bee escapes - making sure that the springs are functioning and not stuck with propolis. An alternative is to use the Canadian cone escapes or, the Hexagonal and Rhombus escapes listed in the bee appliance catalogues. Some beekeepers use Benzaldehyde on an absorbent pad - on a cool day - to drive bees from the supers. When, using clearer boards, the supers, hopefully cleared of bees will be ready for collecting early the following morning. Set out at break of day when things are still cool on the moors. If, left too late, it can suddenly become hot. Then the smell of heather honey will incite the bees into a frenzy and an unnecessary spate of robbing is sparked off. Load the pickup, or van quickly,and depart. There may be some colonies - where the bees have not left the supers - and it will be necessary to shake the bees off the combs; This, is best left until another day, when the bees have settled down and the clearer boards can be removed and the travelling screens - when used - put back on under the roofs and the hives made secure and ready for lifting. This, is best done during daylight hours on some, damp cool day, when all the bees are in their hives and the entrances can again be closed quickly with moss, strips of foam rubber, etc. Never-use bee blowers to get bees out of the supers on the moors - as the stress factor invariably brings about over - wintering problems associated with Nosema.

When the hives are small, with only one super on each, the usual practice is to leave the honey on the hives, and bring them off the moors as they are. Leaving the honey until the first sharp night frost, when the bees leave the supers of their own accord as they go into cluster. The supers can then be lifted off the hives the following morning - clear of bees - after first breaking the seal between the brood chamber and super with the hive tool. Fastening devices are best removed as soon as the hives are brought back to their permanent apiary sites. Should straps be left on hives during the winter, shrinkage can damage hive parts. The entrance blocks with 12 inch wide and 3/8th high apertures will usually deter mice.

Watch that Braula larvae and Wax moth don't ruin the heather comb honey. Honey from the Ling is extremely sensitive to over-heating and freezing so take great care when handling it. Pressing heather honey is a time consuming business but the MG Press introduced by the late Arthur Abbot has invariably given years of sterling service since it appeared 50 years ago. In more recent times, STEELE & BRODIE made a stainless steel water operated Press available. It is essential to have a really good mains pressure water supply for this. Larger producers of heather honey make use of mechanical full frame looseners which enables them to extract the honey tangentially. Smaller producers sometimes use a heather honey roller and spin drier for extraction in a room which is warm and dry, and where, if possible the supers of heather honey have been stored for several days. Heather honey extracted in this way is certainly not as attractive in appearance as that pressed slowly in a MG, Peebles or, STEEL & BRODIE Press.

EXHIBITING HONEY

Both Hamilton and Tinsley give interesting accounts of how to prepare Heather Honey for the Show Bench. While, the well known Exhibitor of honey, the late Bernard Leafe, contributed a fine article on the subject to the 1982 Yorkshire BKA Centenary Handbook.

MARKETING HONEY

Small scale beekeepers usually dispose of their cut- comb and pressed honey to business colleagues who are anxious to obtain such a wonderful natural product, rich in protein, off the hills. Larger producers of heather honey often market their crop through Co-operatives and Packers, or, aggressively sell their product at Country Fairs and Agricultural Shows. Northumberland's first commercial beekeeper Robert Reed, who, worked several hundred skep colonies around Acklington and Morpeth, between 1760 and 1812, was a pioneer in such marketing, attracting large crowds at Fairs as completely unprotected he drove his quiet brown bees from their skeps and then scooped them up with his bare hands to fill empty skeps.

SHRIMP BROOD

One condition of the brood which I have seen on a few occasions during my 50 years of heather-going beekeeping, was first described by the late Bob Couston as SHRIMP BROOD page 72 "THE PRINCIPLES OF PRACTICAL BEEKEEPING" During the months of June, in 1957 and 1962 and early July 1975, there were heavy death rates amongst sealed brood in hundreds of apiaries throughout the East of Scotland. The worst colonies had over a third of the sealed brood affected all of which had died on the 13th or 14th day stage of development, having the body segments formed and the pigment of the eyes just starting. The dead pupae - were quite firm - almost crisp - and were reminiscent of the consistency and appearance of small, freshly cooked peeled shrimps. The affected cells were scattered about in random fashion - some being next to normal pupae of the same age. In all cases, the malady cleared up within a three-week period of the onset of the condition - but, on observing this in their apiaries, many beekeepers became worried because the initial appearance with dark and sometimes perforated cell-cappings - resembled that of A.F.B. The outbreak always followed a poor heather season the year before -and it is interesting to record that not one case of the malady was seen amongst the thousands of stock inspections during the intervening years. There, is certainly an opportunity here for Rothamsted or Sheffield to do some serious work on this.

CONTROL OF "*VARROA DESTRUCTOR*"

The control of this parasitic mite is now an essential part of our beekeeping year. Beekeepers are recommended to read the latest available document advising on its management. This is available from FERA National Bee Unit, Sand Hutton, York, North Yorkshire, YO41 1LZ or it can be read online at >www.nationalbeeunit.com<

LABELLING OF HONEY

With the increased popularity of home computers more people are creating their own honey labels. Labelling is governed by The Honey (England) Regulations 2003 as amended. The last amendments were made in 2007. These specify the wording permitted on labels to describe the honey and the information which must be included such as the name and address of the producer or seller, the country of origin, i.e, Product of UK. The weight in grams, a "best before date" and in some circumstances a "lot number".

If the words "Heather Honey" are used then the honey *must* come wholly or mainly from the indicated source. The term 'mainly' is not defined but tests include moisture and electrical conductivity tests so care must be taken in choosing the wording. Might it be better to use the name of the general location of your heather stance, "Blanchland Honey".

THE ART OF BEEKEEPING
by
WILLIAM HAMILTON

The Art of Beekeeping by William Hamilton was printed and published in compact war-time standard style in February 1945 by The Herald Printing Works, Coney Street, York.

William Hamilton died in 1977 and the copyright now lies with his nephew Graham Hamilton who has kindly given permission for the use of the following chapter.

THE ART OF BEEKEEPING

HEATHER HONEY PRODUCTION

The production of heather honey is quite apart from the production of other honeys. It requires a special study, and only those who have had a lot of experience with it know the difficulties.

DESCRIPTION OF THE HEATHER

The heather (Calluna vulgaris) is a native plant of the British Isles, and other parts of Northern Europe and Asia. As far as Britain is concerned, the best heather grows in Scotland, and naturally the best heather honey is produced in that Country. Large stretches of heather are found, however, in England and Ireland, and the honey, although lacking the fine flavour of Scottish heather is very good.

The heather thrives and seems to yield more and finer nectar on shallow acid soils, derived from igneous and metamorphic rocks, and especially from whinstone and greenstone. Heather requires little moisture, and often the best heather is found on comparatively bare rock. Where it grows on deep peaty land or on wet land, it is almost useless for nectar unless in a time of severe drought.

Although the heather is a hardy plant, and can stand severe cold? the blossom can be badly damaged by late frosts in May, when the buds are forming, and also by early frost in August and September.

A good deal of trouble has been experienced in recent years by the attack of the heather beetle which kills the plant. The browning of the foliage resembles the damage done by frost.

The heather blooms in August and September, usually beginning about the end of the first week in August in early districts and lasting until nearly the end of September in later districts. Much depends on altitude and on the nearness of the sea. Heavy rains after the flower blooms usually wash all the nectar from the flowers, and curtail the blooming period. In mountainous country the best heather is often found growing at from 600 to 1,000 feet above sea level. On the West coast of Scotland the best heather is invariably found from a little above sea level to about 600 feet.

The honey produced from heather is of a brilliant golden amber colour. It is the most viscous of all "honeys and cannot be extracted in the usual way by centrifugal force, and, therefore, is best used as a comb honey. The aroma is at times almost overpowering in its rich fragrance. It has more of the fundamental perfume of flowers than any other honey. Clover honey, or for that matter, any other honey is as a dull day in Winter to a glorious day in Spring compared with heather honey. One feels that he can almost feed on the fragrance and keep drawing in long gulping breaths for ever.

The flavour is like the aroma. Too rich, perhaps, for some delicate palates, but therein lies its goodness, and a little is enough of a good thing. The flavour is pleasant but searching. It is a full flavour with little or no trace of the bitter sweet about it as is so often stated. Some so-called heather honeys are sometimes more of the bitter-sweet variety, but that seldom applies to comb heather honey produced in Scotland.

There is no greater joy than sitting down on a bed of heather and eating the first chunk of warm heather honey straight from the hive. There is no doubt about it that the throat and the stomach too, indicate that here we have indeed nature's finest sweet, and the nectar of the gods. Unfortunately, heather honey is often contaminated from other less desirable sources. Ragwort, that yellow, upstanding daisy-like flower, so often seen in pastures in the Autumn (because the cattle and sheep will not eat it, even when a seedling), produces one of the most bitter of honeys, and it takes very little of this honey to spoil what might have been a splendid sample of heather honey.

DIFFICULTIES OF PRODUCING HEATHER HONEY

Heather honey is seldom an easy crop to obtain in quantity. The weather is often adverse; the colonies are losing strength and difficult to build up; and usually the bees have to be transported long distances. Special preparations have to be made, if a good crop is to be secured.

METHODS OF PREPARING COLONIES

Bee-keepers who specialise in heather honey production often divide their colonies in early Summer by allowing them to swarm, or by artificial division. These divisions with young or old queens are allowed to build up, and are usually in a fair condition by the time the heather blooms. One objection to this system is that the clover or other Summer crop is largely sacrificed and, moreover, these colonies are usually uneven in condition, and often fail to pay their way.

A much better method, not often enough practised, is to unite swarms and casts to make up very strong colonies, just prior to heather blooming. On the other hand, allowing swarms and casts is bad practice. Those bee-keepers who work big colonies in mid-Summer and keep them undivided often take these colonies to the moors without any special preparation, but without any great hope of success. Usually, these kind of colonies are unsatisfactory, unless they have been kept with a brood-chamber of twenty combs all the time, or specially treated.

A method sometimes practised with success is to make up strong lots by uniting or using driven bees and putting on to shallow combs.

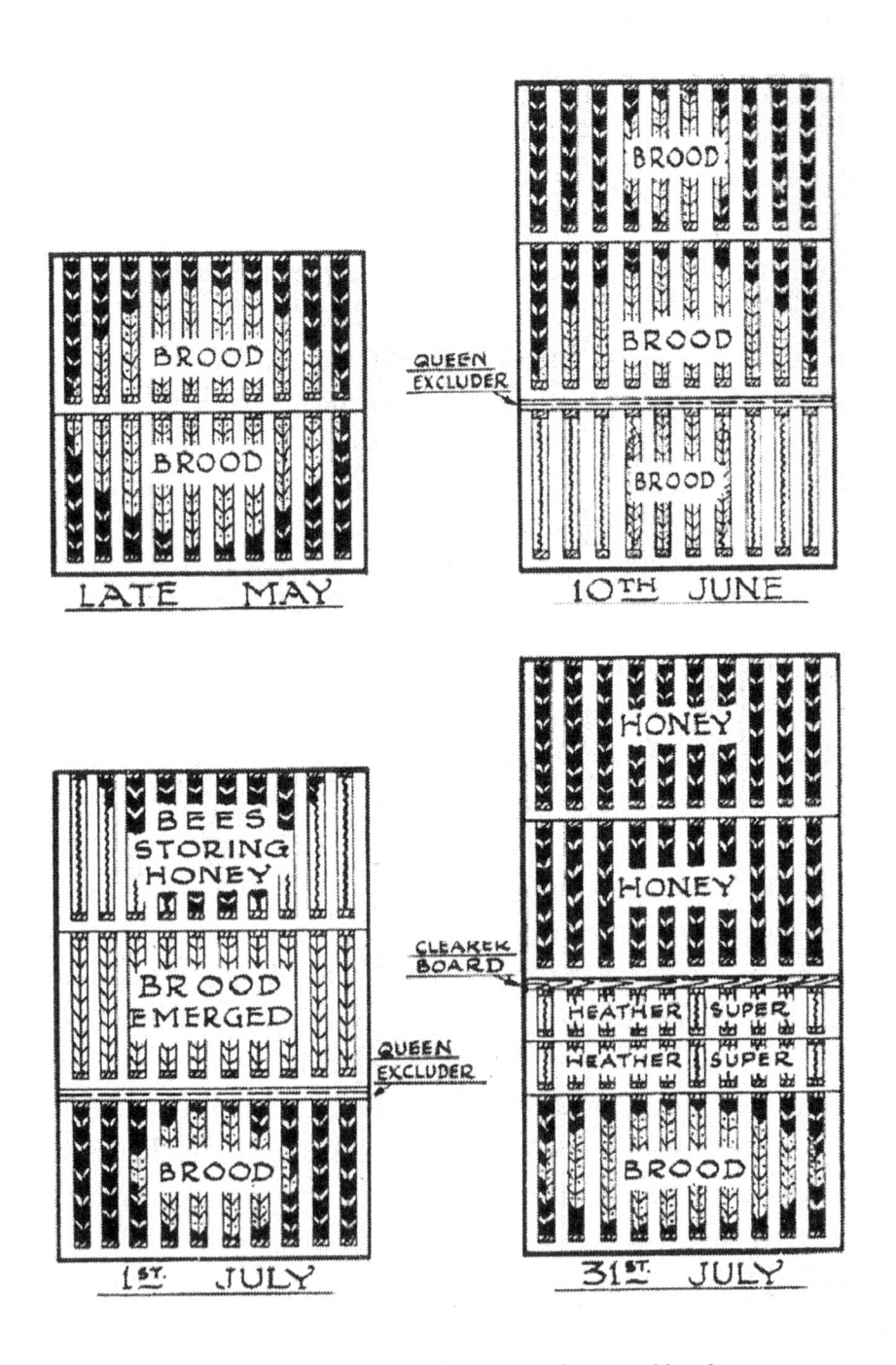

Stages in the production of honey from clover and heather (see text for details).

Probably the best method for the average bee-keeper is as follows:

Early in June, a nucleus should be made from each colony, or one or more colonies can be divided for the purpose. The nucleus should have two combs of sealed brood and enough bees to cover four combs. A ripe queen-cell should be given to each nucleus. Abundance of food and breeding room should be provided, and with careful attention each nucleus should be a good colony on ten or more combs by the beginning of August. The box to hold the nucleus need not be a proper hive, and such things as a brood-box, a travelling box, or even a home-made box of rough timber will suit, so long as it will hold eight to ten combs.

The temptation is strong to take these colonies as they stand to the moors. They should be united, however, one to each of the main colonies in the Apiary. If desired, the old queens in the main colonies can be held in nuclei until the return from the moors when they can be killed, and on the whole this is sound practice, as heather colonies usually need some help for Winter.

The condition of each colony after uniting should be such that there should be about ten combs of brood in each hive and enough bees to need at least twenty combs to hold them. No more than ten combs should be used in the brood-box or the hive will be cumbersome and heavy. But what is more important is that the work in the supers will be affected. Where colonies are not up to the required standard, the brood-box can be contracted to eight combs. The brood can be so arranged at the time of uniting that the younger brood is towards the outside, and the more mature brood in the centre of the brood-box. This has the tendency to prolong the egg laying of the queen, and to force the honey into the supers.

It is advisable to have all uniting done about a week before moving the hives. Supers can then be put in place and time given for packing and adjustment. Queen excluders are not needed for heather working. It is always wise to put a few unfinished sections in the first rack. These can be put at the outside and have the double purpose of providing a food supply in case of emergency, and of coaxing the bees to start work above when the honey comes in. If sections have been partly worked out from earlier flora, more honey will be obtained, especially in a bad season. Where there is a poor market for sections it is much better to use shallow combs for producing pressed heather honey, and often these combs can be marketed without being put through a press. The bees will work foundation as long as it is soft, and in good seasons will do amazingly well with starters of foundation. As a rule two section racks or shallow frame boxes are sufficient to begin with, although, if a long distance has to be travelled, and the colonies are in proper condition, one or two extra may be needed.

Bee-keepers who wish to obtain the maximum crop from clover as well as heather, are advised to try the following system which can hardly be excelled. Towards the middle of June, put the queen excluder between the two boxes of brood as has been described earlier. In the bottom brood-box leave four good combs of brood with the queen, and on each side of the brood place three frames with foundation. This is obviously a modified Demaree plan and has two objects, providing the bees are not already preparing to swarm. Firstly, it tends to prevent swarming, and secondly, it rests the queen as she has only the four brood combs to lay in. The second point is as important as the first. Generally, the bees are slow to work on the foundation in the bottom box and it may be the middle of July before they get the combs built out. However, about the 1st of July the bottom brood-box must be inspected and if the foundation has been neglected it must be taken out and combs put in its place. These combs can be taken from the top brood-box and they may have a little honey or some sealed and emerging brood, or they may be empty. The queen now gets going again after her enforced rest, and obviously a new queen can be introduced if the old queen is not considered satisfactory. The amount of brood in the bottom box steadily increases until at the end of July, the colony is in first rate condition for the heather honey harvest in August. The frames with the unworked foundation are placed in the top brood-box and are soon built out and filled with clover honey in an average season. The surplus brood taken in the first place from the bottom brood-box may be placed in a third brood-box and put on top of the supers, or given to another colony that may need it.

THE HIVE

A suitable hive should be used. Various types and sizes of hives are used for the earlier honey flows, but not many are suited for moving to the moors. A bee-keeper who intends to make a practice of producing heather honey should consider using a general purpose hive like the National or Langstroth types. The hive for heather should be compact. It should have a flat roof, no legs or porch, and a capacity for no more than eleven combs. Ample provision should be made for ventilation in the floorboard during transportation. The supers, especially the section racks, should allow for plenty of warm packing. The joints between the brood-box and the supers should be a perfect fit, whether the hive be double or single walled. A good cover should be provided to seal the tops of the supers, and Celotex board or oil cloth are suitable, also wooden covers and jute cloth. The usual section rack holding twenty-one sections is often too big and may be reduced to hold eighteen or even fifteen sections.

TRANSPORTING THE BEES

The moving of the bees requires much care. The hives should he secured with laths and nails or with suitable wire. Rope is seldom satisfactory unless for short distances. Roofs can be fixed with wood screws. If a long distance has to be travelled no packing should be put over the supers. A piece of porous sacking or a wire-cloth screen is the best cover, but for a short distance the full packing can be put on. The perforated sine in the floor-board should be of ample dimensions. The entrance to the hive should be completely closed with a strip of wood or with grass stuffed tightly. Perforated sine at the entrance of a hive is positively dangerous to the bees, as they crowd against it in their endeavour to escape, and it creates great excitement in the colony. This excitement causes overheating, and shortens the life of the bees by half, if it does not kill them. Even if ample ventilation is given it is unwise to close the entrance of a strong colony until a short time before loading the hive on to the waggons. Many a fine colony has been ruined by closing the entrance, and confining the colony for an hour or two on a warm morning in early August. It is much better to lose some flying bees than risk damage to the colony. The time to move bees to the moors is at night. In darkness the most powerful colony hardly realises it is being moved. In day light big colonies are nearly always overheated and weaker lots often beat them as a result. Perhaps the next best thing is to leave for the moors at dawn (about 5-0 a.m., Summer Time). A motor waggon is obviously the best means of transport, and as many as sixty hives of a suitable type can be taken on a two ton waggon.

THE SITE

The advantages of a good site are obvious. As a rule, not much difficulty should be experienced in finding a good site if one lives within easy reach of the moors, but on the other hand it may take years of search to find a favourable site if one lives at a distance.

A day should be spent in exploring the area where it is intended to take the bees. Much information can be gleaned by getting in touch with shepherds or sheep farmers. The site chosen should be near to a road or good track, but well away from the public highway. A high pasture field or the garden of a forester or shepherd is often available. The ideal location is in a sheltered valley with heather on either side. If possible, the hives should face in an Easterly direction as not only is the morning sun helpful, but the prevailing winds in the Autumn are from the North-West, and a cold night wind blowing into the entrances is not desirable. If the site chosen is half a mile from the heather it is near enough. It should be pointed out that the same site is not necessarily the best every year, as owing to the periodical burning off of the heather at intervals, sometimes intentional and sometime accidental, the amount of suitable heather may vary greatly.

The arrangement of the hives on the site calls for some attention. Bees are much inclined to drift on the moors. The hives should never be placed in a long straight line. A good plan is to place the hives in pairs about two feet apart and to have each pair at least eight feet away from each other. The hives can be placed on short pieces of; wood or on stone, and the entrance kept as near the ground as possible. A board should be laid in front of each hive, to aid the many heavy laden bees that fall or are blown down, just as they are about to enter the hive.

MANAGEMENT AT THE MOORS

Very little work has to be done at the heather. Weekly visits should be paid, and a supply of sections or combs should be provided in the event of fine weather. If insufficient room is provided the bees soon show it by hanging in clusters at the entrances. A good plan, if time permits, is to prise out all finished sections and replace with empty ones. In an indifferent year it is the only safe way. At other times, an extra box can be put on top and generally it is always safer to give extra room on top rather than below. The brood nest should never be disturbed. In some cases, supers may be transferred from one hive to another. If colonies are strong, entrances should be left wide open.

GENERAL NOTES

In some localities there is a considerable amount of Bell Heather (Erica cinerea) and also Cross-leaved Heath (Erica tetralix). These plants usually bloom before the heather (from about mid-July), but the honey is poor in quality compared with heather. The colour is reddish amber, and the honey can be extracted. To the bee-keeper its chief virtue is that it helps to fill up.

Hot weather, or what is generally termed a heat wave in this country, is the best for the secretion of nectar in the heather.

Heather honey keeps better in the comb form than most other honeys. Pressed heather honey loses much of its flavour and is very liable to ferment unless heated to kill the yeasts.

One part of pressed heather honey to four parts of clover makes an excellent blend relished by most people.

Pure heather is slow to granulate in the comb, but often granulates rapidly after pressing. Pure heather honey dripped from the combs seldom shows signs of granulation under nine months. Heather granules are different from other honeys, and are large and of a flint like hardness.

One advantage of taking the bees to the moor is that if they do nothing else they get ample food for Winter. Heather bees seldom need to be fed. Heather honey seems to cause more dysentery during Winter, and sugar feeding is advisable in late September.

Bees working on heather invariably return with the typical grey pollen on their legs. The load is never a large one, but the pollen indicates to the bee-keeper the percentage of bees at work on the heather. When the heather is secreting nectar in quantity there is an abundance of pollen, and in walking through it one's boots get covered with the nectar and pollen. The purple of the heather has more red in it when it is good, and an experienced bee-keeper can tell, even before the bloom opens, what the prospects are likely to be.

POINTS TO REMEMBER

(1) Only strong colonies are profitable on the moors, and plenty of brood is needed up to the beginning of the bloom.

(2) Warm packing over and round about the supers is desirable. But remember this if you remember nothing else, or have time for nothing else.

Plenty of bees—is the best packing.

(3) Small hives are best (ten combs or eight).

(4) Ventilation is most important. Give plenty below and above, when transporting, but not at the entrance of the hive. Remember that many of the bee-keepers who may scoff at this advice, either live on the borders of the moors or do not know what a strong colony of bees is like.

(5) Finally, the weather may be, as it nearly always is, the deciding factor on the size of crop obtained, but there can be no question that the bee-keeper who follows closely the system here outlined will be successful to a large degree. And there will be satisfaction in knowing that the ability to produce good crops on the heather is the best qualification to be a master bee-keeper.

HEATHER HONEY
BY
PETER SCHOLLICK

PREFACE

During my long and happy involvement with bees and honey I have enjoyed many years of exhibiting honey at the annual National Honey Show. There I have had a great many successes to the extent that I have recently been told that I currently hold the record for winning the second most awards in the history of the show.

Briefly these successes include having won all the cups for heather honey, some more than once, and in particular the Burnett Cup which having won it bars you from re-entering that class again. In some years, because I have won so many points at the show I have been instrumental in The Yorkshire BKA winning the Smallholder County Challenge Shield six times.

I have always hoped that my winning of so many trophies would be an inspiration to other Yorkshire beekeepers to enter the show in order to support the considerable efforts that are put into arranging it by a great many people and, if for no other reason, to try to beat me.

The following concentrates more on the heather moors and the many aspects of moorland beekeeping and considerations which have to be made in getting the bees to the heather.

I hope you will find it interesting and instructive.

Peter Schollick.

ACKNOWLEDGEMENTS

I grew up in the 1940's, the WW11 years, father was already keeping bees and there were always bees in the garden. No TV, computer games or mobile phones etc. Yes, I became the helper at a very young age and a few stings here and there did not seem to put me off. Until national service the bees were very much dad's, I became the apprentice so to speak and did or assisted with whatever there was to do as instructed. This proved to have been an excellent period of learning about the craft.

National service behind me, so the bees became mine. I became the decision maker but I did have an overseer. Many times I was given instructions and/or advice but gaining all the while with experience. It has been established that you gave me an excellent start. I probably appreciate that more now than I did then. So thanks Dad.

Bill Reynolds NDB and Bill Bielby***, both noted Harrogate beekeepers took a considerable interest in teaching, encouraging and injecting enthusiasm into my beekeeping. My main development with the craft is thanks to them.

I have been most fortunate to know Br. Adam. He has built on what I already knew from his vast knowledge and experience with a further injection of enthusiasm.

This past fifteen years or so my chief mentor has been Bernard Diaper from the West Midlands. He knew what I was doing and seeking to achieve. He pushed me further by simply saying, "You can do it". I have to admit this has worked. Thank you Bernard.

Eh dad! If only you could know what you started!

I was born in Richmond North Yorkshire in 1938. Father began learning about beekeeping 1938, so I am told, and obtained his first bees in 1940. It follows then that I don't remember not having bees to look after and honey on the table. As a youngster, growing up in the war years, the honey on the table was a key part in the family diet as a result of the shortages in other key food areas.

It also follows therefore that I was the helper. Whenever tasks were necessary I would be involved holding this, passing that, going for whatever to enable the task to be completed. It was to prove to be the start of a lifelong involvement in the craft of beekeeping. If only dad could know today what he had started way back in the late 1940's. You could call it one lifelong apprenticeship for that is what it amounts to. You are in fact learning all the time, season in, season out; realising all seasons differ and adjusting to the changes. With the passage of time trying to recall when those situations occurred in the past and how you responded then and asking yourself will that be the right way this time or is there a better course of action.

THE SEASONS

One of the lessons I was given way back in those early days was that we were particularly fortunate to reside in this part of the country because we were able to enjoy a more or less continuous flow of worthwhile forage sources for the bees from late April until late summer as we were able to take the bees to the heather moors. That is subject to the weather allowing the bees to do whatever they needed to do.

Most of my beekeeping has been undertaken in and around Richmond in North Yorkshire.

We referred these beekeeping seasons to having three main flows. The first "flow" - the end of April to into June covered the trees, mainly sycamore, chestnut and hawthorn and wherever the bees could locate the fruits, soft fruits and early flowers. Oil seed rape was not around then so no problems with granulated honey in combs etc. For the most part sections were used, as securing the use of an extractor was not that easy. There were not many to hand and everyone wanted the use of one at the same time.

There followed what was referred to as the "June gap". A period of about two weeks, with very little significant forage available, waiting for the summer flowers or second "flow" to appear. I recall clover flowers being more readily available in those days. Significant forage sources then included lime trees, the bramble and willow herb along with the summer meadows. Depending on how the season unfolded it was sometimes possible to secure some sections of lime honey. A wonderful honey with such a distinctive flavour of it's own and there was no mistaking this. This period would usually close with the lime flow finishing at the end of July.

For most beekeepers this represented the end of opportunities to secure any surplus honey that season. The bees needed to build up to enable them to winter successfully with some late breeding and indeed sufficient stores for colony survival until the following spring. Usually this was only possible with beekeeper support.

However for those fortunate enough to have heather moors in flying distance of the bees or able to migrate with their colonies to the moors there was a further period or "third" flow available. I am in that category. Some beekeepers with bees located near to heather moors often miss out on an early flow because colonies have not built up sufficiently. This then leaves the heather flow as their main source of surplus honey as it can be available until early September in some seasons. Another significant benefit is that it enables the bees to secure what will probably be most of their winter keep.

This honey from the heather moors is for me, and indeed many others, our "Premier Product". I could however easily be biased. It does have a strong flavour for some and for many it is an acquired taste. A taste that they nevertheless like to keep satisfied.

WORKING FOR A SURPLUS OF HEATHER HONEY

I consider myself to be a hobby beekeeper. Someone who has taken a variable number of colonies to the moors from the early years as assistant to my father up to the present time for my own purposes. For many of those years my arrangements for the whole exercise of carrying through the complete task had to fit around work, family life and looking after parents and their needs. More recently, embracing retirement years, I have been able to focus more precisely on the tasks required and even secure some quality produce that has brought rewards on the show bench at the top level. Almost a double you might say - heather honey and awards.

To make the effort of taking bees to the heather moors a successful one it comes almost as a separate exercise in ones overall bee management. That is quite apart from whether the heather will yield and at the same time will the actual weather permit the bees to do their work. You will appreciate then that I have experienced all situations.

For the most part I have taken my bees to a heather stance on the moors above Leyburn. A location adopted by my late father. It is a south facing area of gently sloping ground with grazing sheep and a magnificent view across Wensleydale as well as up and down the dale. A programme of heather burning is still carried out which ensures that there are areas of new grown heather to provide good bloom and hopefully good yield.

To provide this basically essential bloom the heather plant needs to get off to a good growth each spring. This needs to commence in May to enable sufficient necessary growing time and for this to happen there needs to be a period of reasonable warmth and rainfall. A dry May is usually not conducive to obtaining a good yield come August. It is the springtime growth that produces the amount of bloom.

There comes a time when, whilst working the bees through the summer flow, considerations will need to be made to decide which colonies are going to be worth the effort of transporting to the heather. The basic considerations are a strong colony with a substantive queen, in regular lay, with a good supporting number of flying bees of all ages and with a complete brood box of healthy brood at all stages of development. As a rule of thumb it is good practice to work on the assumption that the heather will start to bloom at the beginning of August. Make no mistake this can and will vary from season to season. I have known this variation be from about the 26th July through to the 12th August. I refer here to the period of bloom starting, which can be very different from the period of yield. It will therefore be appreciated that decisions have had to be made long before it is evident just when the heather will be ready for the bees as to which colonies will be suitable and indeed ready in time. To cover this it may be an advantage to have possible heather bound colonies at different stages of development as this can assist in covering varying flow circumstances.

You will have noted that the dates I have quoted cover a period of almost three weeks. Taking this point alone that is the time it takes for a newly laid egg to hatch or alternately, embrace the flying life cycle of a foraging bee. Factors that can significantly affect how successful your visit to the heather will be.

As with everything, preparation is an all-important. The actual start time is in some ways beneficially timely, as requeening may well have been undertaken or the established queen happily working in her role. This does assist, as there should have been no loss of laying time. These challenging situations are what makes beekeeping what it is. It is also fair to say that luck plays its part. What is luck? One answer could be where and how appropriately preparation meets circumstance! All the while you can be hopeful that the colonies are working the summer flow.

A suitable location for your heather stance will need to be found should one not have already been found for you and which you are able to adapt.

WHAT ARE THE CONSIDERATIONS FOR A GOOD HEATHER STANCE?

The ones that are relevant for any apiary site are applicable. But what you will find is that these are rather more difficult to accommodate making compromises necessary. Easy flying onto the heather. Hives facing early sun with some shelter to the rear of the hives. Maybe a moor boundary wall. Access to enable hives to be placed as near to the position required when they are lifted from the rear of the vehicle. Security - behind a locked gate. It is worth remembering that if they are easy for you to drop off they will also be easy for a thief to collect. They may not necessarily take the hives straight away but wait until there is a harvest of liquid gold on board to make the theft more worthwhile. Given that you are more than likely dealing with open moorland a wall can be handy not only for shelter, but in addition the flying bees will be able to use the wall to follow as a navigation reference to and from the stance location. An area of lower ground may provide some relief from winds and strong breezes, which can have their toll on the amount of flying time the bees have in them.

The flying bees should not be required to cross any local roads or moorland trails or rights of way that could be used by hikers. Selecting your preferred site does not make it yours nor should it have the potential to interfere with another beekeeper. So far so good, however you must have the permission of the landowner and agree any rental costs and be prepared to meet any other requirements that they may have. You may find that all they wish for is none other that some good freshly collected heather honey.

Heather stance selected and agreed. You are likely to find it necessary to prepare the site before you are to take the colonies. Being moorland there could be thistles, nettles, bracken etc. to clear and the same for any access route. The better or more complete the preparation the easier the move will be.

There is the question of do you place the hives in a straight line or randomly to prevent the drifting of the flying bees as they return to their colony. This can happen if they are wearisome with flying against the wind or maybe with a drop in temperature and glad of any port in a storm. They will probably be accepted into another colony, as they are likely to be laden with forage and welcome. My own experience and situation at the heather stance requires that the colonies are placed in a straight line on the leeward side of a stonewall. I have found that no real problem arises as I have a selection of colonies that vary in appearance being both WBC's and Nationals and this gives the returning bees a better chance of locating their colony. The evidence that I have for this is that the colonies that perform the best each season are not necessarily the end ones and they would be if the bees were entering the first hive that they reached at the time of their return flight. For a good deal of the time they use the stonewall that I have referred to as a navigational aid to assist with their return to the stance. It is quite fascinating being able to watch them fly across the moor to the wall and then turn to follow the wall back to the stance.

WHEN IS THE RIGHT TIME TO MOVE TO THE HEATHER MOORS?

The flowering periods for the heather vary from region to region and moor to moor. It becomes necessary to get to know ones heather stance in closer detail. It is also a good time to be able to relate what is happening on the moor to what is happening in the home apiary location. The progression of the season will indicate when flows in the home apiary are coming to an end and there will be a corresponding progression on when the heather will be in bloom and ready to yield. This should enable the beekeeper to determine just when the time is right to make the move. The sort of situation to which I refer is one that generally works for me and was operated by my father so no credit to me for this one. In late July for my area the lime tree blossom has passed its best and ceases to yield. This can, in most seasons, be determined by the flying pattern seen at the hive entrance. The number of flying bees reduces and the flying pattern has less purpose. A kind of idleness is evident. Another foraging plant to watch is the golden rod for activity from the bees to stop. The thing to do is to select a similar situation from your local foraging sources and similarly relate for future reference. Therefore the time is then right to make the move.

WHICH TYPES OF HIVES FOR THE MOOR?

I operate both single and double wall hives. I regularly transport both types to the heather moors. The question which is best or more accurately which type of hive leads to producing the better results is one that is often asked. It is my experience that the answer varies and is usually dependant on the season. Securing heather honey comes at the end of the season as a whole. The days are becoming shorter; the average temperature is falling with the result that the opportunities to forage are declining. For me this means that the bees need all the support that can be provided. I use full floors and, where possible, with the single wall hives I use heather floors. Dare I say Yorkshire heather floors! The design of the heather floor allows the bees a sheltered landing area at the hive entrance. This can also be utilised as a resting area in times of wind and lower than desirable temperatures. It helps to keep the returning bees off the ground at the hive entrance enabling them to enter the hive without taking another short flight that could be prevented by a drop in temperature and hence the loss of bees. From the sheltered landing the bees are able to make their way up a short sloping area, through a narrow bee entrance the width of the hive and into the brood box. This design has two main attributes. One is that the bees have assistance in maintaining the temperature of the hive and secondly the narrow design is easier for the bees to defend from robbing and keeps unwanted vermin out. Being single wall the top of the hive can benefit from the beekeepers assistance. Bedding can be used to help reduce any heat loss through the roof. As the hive is single wall any super has but one layer of protection to the side. A deep lid can provide a second layer. It follows that as the days get shorter the nights get longer and cooler therefore holding onto the temperature already gained is important. If you are buying a lid, better a deep, it may cost a little more, but that extra expense will be repaid in the longer term via increased yields. You will be rewarded.

With regard to double walled hives. Obviously there is much more beehive to both carry and accommodate with transportation requirements. I have now developed; I won't go so far as to claim perfected, a routine, which I use regularly, to move a double walled hive and it works as follows. I remove the lid and outer lifts. This leaves the base, brood box and usually a super or section crate with a crown board cover. This I secure with a surrounding hive strap. This part of the hive is lifted into the vehicle for travel. I then place these lifts over the hive and over the strap. Obviously the lifts are prevented from dropping down to rest on the base by the hive strap. I allow them to travel lightly on the straps and maybe sometimes sit the lid on top. The manoeuvre allows the best utilisation of available space in the vehicle for travel. It is accepted that a double walled hive will take up more space resulting in less units being transported each trip. The real benefit is that a double walled hive comes into its own in cooler temperatures with the potential for greater yields.

So then to provide an answer as to which type of hive provides the best results. Well some years it is the single wall and other times it is the double wall. This is only something we will find out at the end of our seasonal visit to our heather stance. With so many variable factors to bring into consideration it is not easy to determine what brings about any particular result.

PREPARING TO MOVE THE BEES TO THE HEATHER MOORS

As the season unfolds a point is reached when summer flows are coming to an end. The natural progression is to prepare the bees for the proposed migration to ones heather stance. I prefer to keep the honey collected to date separate from the heather flow because of the particular nature of the heather honey. Ling heather honey is thyxatropic and will not spin out of the combs. One is left with three main options in these circumstances: -1) Press out using a specially designed heather press, 2) Spinning out using a converted spin dryer or 3) Eating directly from the comb. This requires previously drawn combs from which honey has been extracted or new foundation to be provided for the bees. In most cases asking the bees to produce late season honey using starter comb is a big ask and, in my view, the bees again need all the support that can reasonably be provided by the beekeeper.

Depending on the strength of the colony the bees will need the space in a super for transportation purposes and this is usually the case with any colony worth taking to the moors. This super can either be a super or a section crate. This normally is adequate for transportation and should the season be sufficiently productive a further crate, or in very rare circumstances, a further crate still, can be added as progress requires and indeed a pleasant problem to have. As part of the overall preparation honeys secured to date will be removed and a full check of the brood box made.

For me, a full check at this stage of the season is most important. It may be my last chance to inspect as part of my overall beekeeping practice. Any tendency to swarm will normally have passed. The queen that I am proposing to use to take the colony through the coming winter will be in place and hopefully in regular lay as peak laying will have passed. I will be looking for a good strength of flying bees, brood in all stages of development and stores for current consumption in the flank combs to cover the period of transit. It is my normal practice to use a queen excluder. There is a school of thought that says leave off the excluder to enable the bees, and the queen if she chooses, to have unhindered access to the area above the brood box. In some seasons I have found that leaving the excluder off can result in an extension of the brood nest and this is not helpful when the objective is to secure heather honey. Furthermore it is not good practice to have honey in comb from which bees have been hatched. Should the bees be producing bees they are not foraging for the precious heather honey you are looking to secure. A colony prepared as outlined is as light as it can reasonably be expected for lifting and transportation purposes. Should the opportunity present itself I will remove the queen excluder when sufficient honey has been placed in the super combs thus denying the queen any space to lay.

In some cases where you have sufficient bees but maybe some capacity to increase the brood area sealed brood combs can be transferred in. This should help to bolster the flying force of bees when on the moor.

TRANSPORTATION

Any vehicle or trailer can be used. The question is what is likely to be the best for the bees. The best option is likely to be in the back of a car; preferably an estate car or one with a tailgate. The main reason for this selection is that being a passenger car it is likely to have the softer suspension. Whilst the bees will be aware of the vibration of the travelling vehicle that the hive is on the move they will hopefully not become too distressed. A van or flat back can be less desirable. The principal reason for this is that they are, by their very nature, designed for commercial purposes and will, have heavier springing giving the cargo of hive or hives a rougher journey in addition to reacting less favourably to road surface variations. Less desirable still is a trailer behind any vehicle. They usually move with greater bounce than the towing vehicle as well as having side-to-side movement. The possible adverse consequences of a less than smooth move can lead to the queen being balled. A balled queen is surrounded by the bees and suffocated and consequently lost. Given the timing of this there is little or no time in the season for her to be replaced. Now should this problem arise you are unlikely to be aware of it until during the winter or next spring when the colony fails through being queenless.

Another important consideration, and this applies any time a colony is transported, is to load the hive with the frames pointing in the direction of travel. The reason for this is to eliminate comb slap. This can arise when a hive is moved and should the frames, anywhere in the hive, be allowed to swing from side to side it can cause bees to be crushed, sealed brood to have the capping damaged, in addition to any cells being ruined by swinging together. This is quite important and well worth remembering.

The beekeeper is looking to complete this part of placing the hives on the heather moors as quickly and efficiently as possible. You will have two main choices when it comes to the timing of transporting the bees. The first is to wait until the days flying has ceased or secondly the early morning shift when you will need to be up and moving before the bees. At the end of July or early August this can be rather early. A colony can be secured with hive straps and made ready at leisure during the day so to speak leaving only the entrance to close off at the last minute when the flying ends for the day. It may be appropriate to use a travelling screen should a long journey be contemplated. To close the entrances it is usual to use slides, blocks, foam or cloths etc. That achieved, and usually with another pair of willing hands available, lifting hives into the transport for the move can begin.

In all cases when hive entrances are closed down it is necessary to leave adequate levels of ventilation for the proposed journey.

After the end of days flying, by the time you have reached the moor, any daylight will, for the most part, have gone leaving minimal time to complete the off loading as quickly and easily as possible. As a result of the journey and inevitable vibration the bees will know that they are captive and any delay may not be good. In their anxiety they may build up heat and there is the possibility of balling the queen. Having unloaded then allow a short period for the bees to settle down. You may find that the hives have not been placed on level ground or hive stands. If time permits then take a moment or two to place a stone or block of wood under the lower part of the hive or hive stand until you have them level. It is also good practice to allow some air to pass under the hives to help with keeping the bases dry. Should you not have them level the bees may well not mind and you may or may not. I have to say that I much prefer to see them level. It makes them look right. Should you find that you are unable to do this now you should be able to complete the task at your next visit. That said and done you may find the moorland on the soft side in places and that with the weight of the hive there will be settlement and a further exercise could be required to bring them level.

With the hive levelling completed and suitable bee protection in place it is time to open the hive entrances so releasing the bees. Sometimes an end of day move will be possible on a good summers evening before it is completely dark.

By this time however the daylight will have been lost, or it too dark for the bees to fly. Some bees will come out of the hive entrance, walk around without taking to the wing, before returning back into the colony. Usually they soon settle down and await the dawn.

An early start means being up very early to beat the dawn and the early fliers to close the hive. With any early day move you will be doing it in daylight leading to the fastened in bees becoming increasingly angry and frustrated. In addition once on the move with the bees they are more than ready to leave the hive. You may find that you are rushed to complete the unloading to reduce their and maybe your anxiety. The bees are usually clamouring to be released and it can take a while for them to settle on release before embarking on the reason for the move - foraging for heather honey.

When releasing bees in daylight allowing them to fly out it is advisable to move the vehicle that they have been unloaded from away from the hives. The flying bees will take up quite an extensive flying area until they settle down. This period allows them an orientation flight following relocation.

Sometimes there can be sheep sharing the use of the moor. They have very little scope to rub against fencing or posts etc. It can also be very windy at times. A hive strap can be very useful to keep lids on or prevent hives splitting apart when being rubbed against by the sheep.

The move to the heather complete the success of the exercise is, for the most part, out of your hands. Much will depend on the weather and how and when the heather yields.

THE EARLY PERIOD OF THE HEATHER STANCE VISIT

With a completely new flow available colonies should have a new lease of life. The bees will have recognised the shortening days. All being well they should prove to be queen right following the move. Almost invariably one of the first tasks for the bees is to cull out all the drones as they can be of no useful purpose at this stage of the season. The initial sight of a pile of dead bees on the ground near the hive entrance can be of concern but on closer inspection they should hopefully turn out to be culled drones that have been removed from the hive as far as the bees themselves could take them.

Not all visits to the heather moors go to plan. Our desire for some honey on the moors can coincide with a spell of adverse weather which may well prevent foraging taking place. A colony fit for the moors usually has many mouths to feed, larvae to attend and a queen that needs to be kept in lay. With so much seemingly plentiful forage around starvation can still occur hence the need to be aware of this. Feeding may be required. Care is also required to ensure that any heather honey does not become mixed with any support feeding. There is always something to be mindful of!

Hive entrance slides or in some cases entrance blocks are set to meet the needs of the flying bees. The aim is to permit access for the bees to come and go without struggling to pass each other. There is the need to assist the bees with maintaining hive temperature to enable forage to be accumulated and not spent on their housekeeping needs.

A part of the bee's recognition that the season is drawing to a close is that you will find the early income into the hive is stored in the brood box. As hatching and queen lay is reduced, vacated brood cells are filled with pollen and nectar. This forage is the colonies winter support and for use next spring with the development of the colony. This is likely to begin in the brood box before any new seasons sources can be collected from.

ON THE MOOR - FORAGING FOR THE HEATHER HONEY

The hives are set for foraging and we patiently wait for this to happen. As beekeepers we are eternally optimistic are we not as we await the bees to go about what bees do. I usually check that all is well from time to time. The hives standing as they should and flying in line with the conditions such as yield and temperature. There is always the tendency to visit on a fine day. Should the conditions not be so favourable it can nevertheless be interesting and at times surprising to find just how well they are working at relatively low temperatures. They know working days are becoming fewer and shorter. But this can have its toll on the bees. They may well go to forming part of the winter cluster with little flying mileage remaining for the spring. This can lead to a slow build up for the colony.

FORAGING OVER FOR THE SEASON

Whilst the timing of this will vary from season to season you will know from the state of the moor that the bees have done all they can. There will be patches of brown dead heather amongst the late flowering areas. Flying will be minimal.

With any luck the hives should be rather heavy. Too heavy to lift and transport. To ease this task the honey can be collected from the hives.

It is at this time that I place clearer boards on the hives. Some boards having one others two porter bee escapes. I check that they are working as they should. When placing the boards with the escapes it is most important to ensure the board is completely set so as to cover the bees in the brood box and in turn preventing the bees any way out other than via the bee escapes. The supers, section crates etc. must be totally bee proof. Should they not be then all the honey in them will be removed by the bees. These bees may not necessarily be from the same colony but what they will do with certainty is find a new home for the honey. It will be where they can use it and not where you can use it. Fighting usually takes place with losses that certainly need to be avoided.

It is usual to allow at least two days for the bees to clear the supers. With little flying bee movements within the hive are slow with the bees joining the queen in the brood box. When you return to the moor to collect the harvest you need to know that the supers are likely to be bee free and ready to take off the hive.

Hopefully the crates of honey can be removed into transport for home. This is best undertaken when the weather is not good or at the end of the day. A task to be completed discreetly and if at all possible without disturbing the bees. Should they become aware of what you are doing they will, for certain, make a determined attempt to recover the honey you are taking from them. The situation can become rather messy as they set about uncapping the cells and so spoiling the appearance of the completed combs. There will be robbing bees everywhere. You have been warned!

ENJOY THE HEATHER MOORS

It is my experience that virtually all beekeepers are very fond of the great outdoors. I find that it is not only the bees that can enjoy the heather moors you the beekeeper can do so as well. On a fine day in summer with the heather in full bloom there are few better places.

Perhaps the first thing to occur to you is the peace and quiet on offer. No crowds to contend with; just you and whatever nature has on offer. You will not be disappointed. Time to take in the view in all directions. For the most part this will be heather in bloom. My father would always refer to this as the great untapped. Referring of course to the vast amount of brilliant blooming heather on offer with so few bees to take full advantage. So much possible available forage for the bees, both pollen and nectar.

In the distance the faint sound of motor traffic as both the locals and tourists go on their way.

There will also be the sights and sounds of the moorland bird life. These will be, for the most part different species from those found in your home garden or out apiary. A skylark singing as it climbs skywards as only they can. The call of a passing curlew or two or maybe even more and the very distinguishable rattle call of the native grouse as they move from one feeding spot to another. It doesn't end there. A look high into the sky you may well spot birds of prey riding the warm air currents in search of food. These could well be buzzards or hen harriers in search of carrion to feed their growing broods. Well above them I will be surprised if you do not spot the almost inevitable contrail with the plane at the head and, if it is reasonably calm, the noise of the aircraft itself.

There is the opportunity to pause a while to sit or lie amongst the heather. In the peace and quiet that surrounds you. After a little while it can be surprising the variety of wild life that becomes visible around you. There will be the rabbits of all ages reappearing from their burrows or from hiding amongst the heather. Perhaps an occasional hare moving about checking out their preferred eating stations oblivious to your presence. It does not end there. I have often seen stoat, weasel, mice and even moles making their way over the surface of the ground, and occasionally even in daylight a hill fox on the prowl.

Here and there you are likely to come across the odd patch of thistle and nettle. Just as the heather is in full bloom they are likely to be there too. Contributing in their way to supporting the butterflies, bumblebees, insects and flies that make the moors their home. And surprise surprise you may well find in addition there could even be some of your own honeybees taking a share of whatever is on offer. I always find it wonderful to behold this variety of life that is able to survive for the whole of the year in what is seemingly a most unlikely place. There will be some rarer varieties of butterfly for you to see in addition to those you will be familiar with at home.

I usually find that I feel that I am missing out if I don't linger a while just simply to enjoy the location and all that it has to offer. When all is said and done these are likely to be opportunities that would pass you by were you not going to the moors to check out the bees.

A MOORS BONUS NUMBER ONE

A fine day, a light breeze, the heather in full bloom and most importantly yielding you will be amazed at the spectacle before you. The air full of bees flying to and fro and foraging with such purpose. If only all days on the moor were like this for them and even that these days would never end. The bees are of course well aware that the days are shortening. Foraging time each day is less and they are all too well aware of the need to make the most of available foraging time. Somehow they seem to work with a greater energy and purpose whilst on the moor compared to similar working conditions in the home apiary.

This amazing spectacle that I have referred to coupled with the aroma of the heather bloom is well worth witnessing. To be able to see the flight patterns against the heather back drop, some returning bees laden low over the heather whilst others, outward bound, tend to take a higher route. In some ways this is a form of natural flight control. Those returning are able to make a direct beeline to the entrance of their own colony and no time is lost. Maybe time for more foraging missions.

Whilst watching this action by the bees it can be interesting to note how the bees follow the relief of the moors and where there is a wall they will fly towards it and follow the wall back the location of the hives. This is of course an exercise you can do much more easily in a moors location.

A MOORS BONUS NUMBER TWO

Once the colonies have been on the moor with sufficient time for foraging to take place it is a wonderful experience to wander past the back of the colonies and take in the full blast of the aroma generated by the heather honey actually within the hives. This blast of aroma is even much stronger at evening time. Flying for the day is coming to an end there will be a collection of bees at the hive entrance fanning to assist with the control of the temperature within and of course with the ripening of the secured harvest. Depending upon the success of the day there will be a quite loud hum of contentment and this is best heard by placing your ear as near as is practical to the hive entrances.

Should you live away from the heather stance and only have the opportunity to visit on an evening and have been wondering what sort of foraging day the bees have had then this can be a useful indicator for you. A note of caution, provided you are satisfied that the bees have sufficient room to meet the scope of the foraging, it is best if you can resist the temptation to peep into the colonies as this will result in the loss of temperature. This temperature that they have worked so hard to secure is needed both to ripen the collected nectar and to assist with the wax making for capping. A useful point to mention here is that the collected honey is placed at first in the centre of the super. As more is secured this can only be placed away from the hive centre, away from over the brood nest area, and this area will be cooler for the bees to work anyway. The more that is collected the further it is placed away from the warmer area within the hive. This issue relates to the benefits of single wall hive against those of a double walled hive, the use of full or open floors and the merits of the use of bedding on the top super under the lid and covered elsewhere.

BENEFITS OF THE BEES WORKING FOR HEATHER HONEY

It may not be appreciated by many that there are additional benefits to taking bees to the heather moors to possibly secure some surplus honey and winter keep for our bees. The work of the bees plays an additional part in the life of the moor. Their pollinating efforts generate seeds for the grouse and other moorland bird life. The grouse numbers produced attracts shooting parties. These shooting parties in turn generate valuable income which in due turn is needed to maintain the basic structure and well being of the moor. One of the essential seasonal tasks is heather burning. This involves the burning by rotation of areas of old heather bushes that have become woody and, as a consequence, produce less bloom. This burning allows areas of new heather to grow and become established returning these areas to desired blooming and yielding levels. This exercise involves the burning of seven year old bushes and takes place at designated times in the autumn and spring. In the spring this must be accomplished before bird nesting is under way.

VARIATIONS EXPERIENCED WHEN WORKING FOR HEATHER HONEY

It is probably a fact of life to state that every season is different. This is certainly the case with the heather moors. Perhaps the most obvious variation experienced is the differences in the times of the heather blooming. This is often in line with other seasons being early or late. It may seem extreme but this can vary by almost a month depending on the year. In fact this can be anytime from the third week in July to as late as the third week in August. Of recent the start of the heather blooming has tended to be later. A late start to the blooming does not always lead to it blooming later and this can result in a very short period of nectar and pollen flow. At one time the end of August signalled the end of the flow but recently heather yielding has been noted up to mid September. Does this give the bees a shorter winter?

The period during which the heather yields does often vary. Some schools of opinion say this lasts from as little as a few days to two or three weeks. Another variation is the colour of the honey both from season to season and moor to moor. This in turn leads to a variation in colour, taste and viscosity. Most of us are familiar with the very distinctive golden brown colour which in turn looks very appetising both in the comb and when pressed out into the jar, especially when it has been freshly obtained. To look through the new honey in the jar past the bubbles resulting from pressing out, is for me, one of the most rewarding sights in beekeeping. That is without tasting it. There can be little wonder then to doubt why it is so often referred to as "Our premier product".

To comment on the variations in taste. Whilst there can be no doubting its most distinctive flavour; for many it is an acquired taste, it can vary from maybe being described as a little mild and not particularly viscous to very strong and very viscous. Even from the same location the colour can vary from quite light to rather on the dark side. As beekeepers we are usually pleased with whatever colour it turns out to be as it is something over which we have no control. There can be colour variations from all locations from season to season.

For some the taste of the heather honey proves to be too strong. A way round this is to blend a portion of heather honey with various portions of other honeys. The resultant blend usually proves to be very popular as it provides the taste of the heather honey not quite so strong. The taste of the heather honey will usually still be the dominant flavour, hence its popularity.

I feel it is quite normal to wonder if your moor is yielding as well as the moor being used by another beekeeper. This is in fact something I often wonder about with all my apiary sites. This variance is likely to be the case and most certainly will vary over different parts of the British Isles from season to season. This will average out and I can confirm from my own first hand experience this to be the reality.

POSSIBLE OCCURRENCES WHILST THE BEES ARE ON THE MOORS

With regard to the state of the queen it is recognised that supercedures can take place both early and late season. With late season produced queens this can well take place without the beekeeper knowing about it. Mating can well take place from late hatching drones. The only way you are going to know for certain if this has been the case with you is if you go to the moors with a marked queen and at the time of the following spring inspection you find a queen which has clearly never been marked.

I referred earlier to the worker bees culling out the drones when the colonies are first placed on the moors. There can be a further batch of drone culling at the end of August when the late-hatched drones are cleared out.

HEATHER AND ITS HARVEST

Types of Heather Plant:

1) Ling Heather (Calluna Vulgaris)
This is the main heather plant and the one that we are most familiar with. Covering vast swathes of moorland on the Pennine Ranges and the North York Moors. In the North of England these areas extend from the Scottish Border in the north to Derbyshire in the south. The areas that I am most familiar with are the Pennines in North Yorkshire and on the North York Moors. The plant itself is a coarse bush which doesn't grow very high. When blooming usually from late July and on into September and it can vary from a lightish

pink through to a darkish red. When viewed as one, it is usually referred to as the bonnie purple heather and unmistakeable. The honey secured by the bees from the ling heather can differ in colour from season to season and has a very strong distinctive flavour. The most significant characteristic is that it is thixotropic. Unlike other honeys it is a gel and will not extract no matter how fast the extractor is spun.

2) Bell Heather. (Erica Cinerea)

This normally flowers in late July and is likely to be found in considerably smaller areas. The bloom is a darker red than that of the ling heather. It is rarely worked in this part of the country. Whilst it flowers in late July this period can coincide with other foraging sources. Should it be worked in these small areas it can result in other forage being worked by the bees simultaneously with the resultant blend of honeys. It is a liquid honey, usually very dark red in colour with an almost honeydew appearance. Lacking the thixotropic characteristic of the ling heather it can be extracted normally.

MY METHODS FOR WORKING THE BEES TO OBTAIN THE HEATHER HONEY

You will have noted that I use both single wall and double walled hives. The single walled hives will mostly have heather floors. The hives I operate both use the same frames and sections internally. This means I have no problem with size selection. Between the colonies I will go for a selection of super crates, square sections in crates of 21, 24 or 32 or round sections on the single wall hives in either a 36 or a 40 crate.

Depending on the season if I have been able to manage it I will, on one colony, use a deep super of brood combs that have been drawn, filled and extracted. It will have been returned to the bees temporarily for them to lick it clear of the residue honey. This is to remove any honey that may have a tendency to granulate such as rape honey. It is preferable to do this to ensure that any heather honey is not seeded for granulation and spoil it as heather honey. I am aiming to satisfy one of my self-set challenges by seeking to obtain a fully sealed brood comb. This would be fully capped by the bees on both sides down to each corner with that beautiful white capping characteristic of heather honey. I have been close to success so many times that I am prepared to keep trying. Otherwise it makes good cut comb.

WORKING FOR HEATHER HONEY OR HEATHER BLEND

The main objective of taking bees to the moors is to obtain a surplus of heather honey. This should be the principal consideration when selecting your proposed heather stance. However this may not prove to be as easy as you may anticipate. Bees are capable of foraging up to three miles in any one direction. A stance surrounded with heather for that distance with a workable access is likely to be very difficult to locate. This is without bringing any other considerations on apiary sites into the picture. Your selected site will be governed primarily by access. This in turn will almost certainly have other foraging locations within reach. Where does this leave the beekeeper you may well enquire?

Fortunately for the beekeepers the bees will be keen to work the heather even at temperatures lower than may be expected. Should the heather not be yielding they may locate a nearby plantation of evergreens, a home for aphids and a source of honeydew. This leaves the honey looking muddy coloured and not having the clear gel appearance that you are hoping for. Not the preferred end product for market or even show bench. Other attractions for the foragers could be late flowering lime trees, late clover, Himalayan balsam; a recently encountered invasive plant, late flowering borage and willow herb. Honey from these additional sources will provide you with a natural heather blend.

HONEYS OBTAINED AND MY METHODS OF DEALING WITH ANY CROP

Honey in super combs and square sections can be eaten as it is. Most people can eat the wax without any problems. There is demand for full super combs even if they contain the odd cell of pollen. The frames can be found on hotel breakfast bars for the guests to cut at and eat on their toast. Comb can be divided to make up cut comb cartons enabling consumers to obtain the honey in smaller quantities of say eight or twelve ounces. The sections are popular for handing on as a small gift or acknowledgement of a favour with many ending up as part of a hamper. A section that is not completely filled can be cut down and made into cut comb. The off cuts can go into the pressings or into the blending process.

I referred earlier to the three ways usually used to separate the honey from the comb. The usual method is to use a heather press with the pressure forcing the honey through a muslin cloth or comparable filter. As a result the honey thus pressed, and depending on the size of the gauge produces characteristics bubbles in the honey. These bubbles can vary in size and can easily be seen. Because of the thixotropic nature of the honey these bubbles will remain where they are and will not float up to the surface, as is the norm with other honeys. Ideally it should be clear and you should be able to see well into it and even through it depending on the size of the jar in use. This then is the classic appearance of a good sample of our wonderful golden brown heather honey.

The other methods, spinning out needs the use of an adapted spin dryer, or by using a Norwegian Heather Press, leaving the honey with a less appealing appearance, which is not as clear. These methods do not adversely affect the quality of the honey itself.

With each of these methods of handling the honey becomes liquid for a short time enabling it to run. Once filtered and bottled it soon returns to its gel like state.

Another feature of the heather honey having referred to it earlier as containing bubbles of varying sizes is that a pound measure will not fit into a standard one-pound honey jar. The obvious reason being that the bubbles take up the extra space required. To cater for this we have what we call a heather honey jar. It is taller, albeit slightly, with a less sloping shoulder to the jar. Their use is in decline and to my present knowledge they are not currently readily available.

There will be the unripe honey, the combs with areas of stored pollen in addition to the cut comb off-cuts. These I am able to put to good use. These are used in portions of approximately one third, with a third of granulated and the final third of other honeys in comb which I blend together. Any honey in combs which cannot be used for any other purpose I blend together separating out the wax and pollen by slightly warming. This also enables the granulated honey to be incorporated. Filtered and bottled the resultant blend is very popular. The heather flavour dominates without being too strong and is very spreadable.

SQUARE SECTIONS AND ROUND SECTIONS

Full sections are removed from the crate, cleaned, batch weighed, and boxed or clear wrapped as required. A good square section can weigh as much as 18ozs. gross. Their approximate weight is usually about 1lb. Some, which can look complete, may weigh as little as 12ozs. gross. The reason for this is they are likely to not be completely drawn out even though they will have been capped over by the bees. A result of the available foraging coming to an end.

Round sections fully sealed can weigh anything up to 300g. gross (over 10 ½ oz.) This is well in excess of the 227g quoted on the seal wrapper for the round sections.

Any used section woods I clean up, insert a new piece of foundation and return to the bees. These sections have lost their aroma of new wood and I find the bees move into the crate much more readily and are worked sooner as they have been on the hive previously. The section is also more likely to be filled to meet the wood helping it to make the approximate weight of 1lb as intended. The outside edge of an outer section in the crate is, more often than not, not completed. Being the farthest area from the warmth it is not easy for the wax makers to complete.

COLONIES THAT HAVE BEEN ON THE MOORS

With shortening days the brood area will have been reduced and hopefully this will have been replaced by winter stores. The bees usually winter well on heather stores which may need a little topping up in some seasons. By removing the heather crop before moving the colonies to home apiaries the bees have the opportunity to seal down for winter.

It is not unusual for the later days on the moor to be cooler and windier. I find this can have its toll on colony population numbers as the bees work all they can. Many bees go into the winter with not a lot of mileage left in them. Whilst they are able to support the colony through the winter when spring arrives they can have but a short flying time remaining.

These moor-tired bees can soon be lost as they are worn out. I find the main consequence of this can be that these colonies are slower to build up when compared to ones that have remained away from the moor.

So to conclude. Working for heather honey, as with anything rewarding, is not usually easy. It wouldn't be rewarding if it were. I've not been disappointed, I don't consider you will be.

OVERVIEW FROM BEE BOOKS AND RELATED PUBLICATIONS

As part of our beekeeping learning I am sure many of you will have read and seen photographs of some of the achievements by our predecessors. I have to say that I find these to be quite awesome and indeed even inspiring. Notes of quite seemingly unachievable yields obtained. Filled supers and sections beautiful to behold. Let us take a step back in our thinking and just consider the scale of the preparation that has gone into bringing this about. The size of the colonies, the logistics of transportation, the yield of the heather moor, how fortunate were they with the weather, do they do this every year? I doubt it! But what it does do, or it does for me is show me what is possible and give me every encouragement. It tells me that these bee masters knew a thing or two, in addition to a vast depth of knowledge and experience and they were not afraid of hard work with long hours. Their rewards were not easily earned yet well deserved. As a result I for one am appreciative of all that I can learn from them. As with most things there can be no substitute for experience.

As I relate their efforts and achievements to the present day with our current lifestyles we somehow do not appear to have what it takes to match their successes. There is still a plentiful demand for this quite wonderful product of heather honey and yet we don't work to secure more.

The heather moors are today still and likely to remain for the foreseeable future from the beekeepers prospective as my father called them - "The great untapped". I am sure we know exactly just what he meant.